IN-HER
Rage

FROM PAIN TO PURPOSE

S . L .   B A K E R

ISBN 978-1-0980-5407-6 (paperback)
ISBN 978-1-0980-5408-3 (digital)

Christian Faith Publishing, Inc.
832 Park Avenue
Meadville, PA 16335
www.christianfaithpublishing.com

In-Her Rage is a work of creative non-fiction writings based on a combination of facts about the author's life and certain embellishments. Names, dates, places, demographics, events, and other details have been changed, invented, and altered for literary effect.

Printed in the United States of America

To parents all over the world, especially mothers.
The purpose of this book is to educate, encourage, and enrich.
It is not intended to judge, instill fear or guilt. This book deals
with childhood sexual abuse, abortion, homicide, suicide,
and other traumatic events. Reader discretion is advised.

In memory of my loving mother, *Edna (Vickie) Baker* (April 19,
1930–August 7, 1986). A devoted humanitarian, who dedicated
her life to enriching the lives of others, especially her children.

Acknowledgments

My friends and family call me Bree or Princess. I grew up in the City of Detroit. Growing up in a large metropolitan area had its ups and downs, like any other city. Having a strong family made all the difference in the world.

I'm so grateful for all the teachings my mother provided, and I can now appreciate her struggles as a *single female head of household*. She had a tough job raising me and my two brothers, Draython (Dray) and Anthony (Tony), with a limited support system. My brothers were my hero's and I love them to the moon and back.

I also have much gratitude and love for my paternal grandfather (Grandpa), who adopted Mama as his own from the very beginning. He was a great man in our lives.

Although my relationship with my father was short lived due to his untimely death, he will forever be remembered in my heart.

We had a very close-knit family, and I am humbled knowing that growing up was much easier having strong family members in our home. This includes my aunts Sarah, Mary and Dee; Uncle Robert (a.k.a. Bob); and my cousins, Margaret and Sharon.

Most of all, my inspiration and encouragement to write this book came from my two daughters, Shay and Cierra. From their very conception, they kept me encouraged and gave me the strength to fight for life, even when I felt like giving up.

Sue and Liz, you are my best friends who became my sisters. We are connected for life and I love you both dearly. Harry, you will always be my brother from another mother. Momma Garwood, thank you for standing in the gap. Beth (Bee), you were a rock and taken from us way too soon. You are truly missed.

There are so many others that are too numerous to name, who loved and supported me, consciously or unconsciously, to rise above my circumstances and press forward. I'm so humbled!

Introduction

In-Her Rage (pronounced inner) isn't your typical faith-based book, and is not geared toward those who are walking strongly in their faith. It's specifically for those who've not yet come into the fold, have lost their way while in the fold, or those who have experienced trauma and hurt so deep that it led to the conclusion that God doesn't exist.

It is my sincere hope for this book to become an educational tool that opens the channels of communication for children, families, and communities everywhere. We must do a better job of providing our children and others with a voice that empowers them to be strong and courageous.

With that said, *keeping it real* is all I know. You will ultimately come to your own conclusions as the events of this book unravel, become real, and relatable.

I was known as a *good girl* before child sexual abuse, betrayal, failure, and tragedy led me down a path of self-destruction. It took a long road for me to get to a place of strength and purpose. I want to help others find their path and maybe prevent some of the poor choices and bad decisions I made.

My story is not unique. Everyone has an individualized journey that determines where they end up in life. The road we take frequently has twists and turns. This often causes much pain, anger, bitterness, and growth, which represents the situations of too many women, men, children, families, and communities. My family's tragic journey started prior to me and my brothers being born.

Mama's parents were deceased before she had children, and for most of our childhood she was estranged from seven (7) of her ten

7

(10) siblings. Uncle Bob and Aunt Sarah were always a part of our lives and, for the most part, shared a two-family flat with us.

As the story goes, one brother was killed in a fire, another poisoned by his mistress, an older sister banished from the family, and several siblings separated and estranged early in young adulthood.

I recall Mama hiring a private investigator to locate her siblings. She spent a lot of money, only to be told their whereabouts were unknown. That is until Mama miraculously bumped into one of her sisters, Mary, at the neighborhood grocery store.

How was it possible that after leaving the state of Georgia for more than thirty years, they ended up in the same state, same city, and same community? My mother and aunt resided less than three minutes away from each other, yet a bonded and licensed investigator was unable to locate her? Guess that detective didn't know who he was messing with. She got back every penny.

My mom was a strong and tough woman, as many mothers had to be in my neighborhood. She was a force to be reckoned with and had strict standards for me and my brothers. I didn't understand it at the time, but she was trying to prepare us for the challenges of this world. A place full of good and evil. She tried to expose us to positive experiences but also knew we'd eventually come in contact with some of life's negative influences and wanted to arm us with knowledge.

Like many other parents, Mama wanted the best for her children. Church and education was an expectation, not an option. Disrespect, whether verbal or nonverbal, was not tolerated.

The struggle was real raising two black sons. There was a fear that the streets were waiting with open arms to welcome them to a life of crime. Then there was me, the youngest and only girl. How was she going to keep me safe? How would she protect me from some of the tragedies she herself had experienced? It wasn't about living in Detroit, but about surviving life.

Looking back on my childhood, I'm reminded of all the good times we shared in our home. A place full of joy, laughter, and holidays to live for.

I grew up in a community where two-family homes were the standard. Multiple generations banned together in one house as a means for survival. Our family was no different.

The children in our home were fortunate to have a hot breakfast prepared for us every morning and great dinners each evening. There were Thanksgiving-style dinners almost every Sunday, and we never had to miss a meal. Not all families were so fortunate, and not every child had enough to eat.

Yes, there were a lot of good times, but bad times were always lurking around the corner. Mama, along with many other single mothers, and two-parent households, were challenged with steering children in the right direction. Unfortunately, even the most involved parents can lose the battle against peer pressure, the need to be accepted, and the desire to have more money and things. Often times their only hope was fervent prayer and belief that God was omnipresent (everywhere) at all times.

Negative peer influences is what happened with Tony, my oldest brother. Sometimes a parent's love is just not enough. No matter how hard they tried.

Tony was a hilarious character and set the standard for what not to do. He was about 6'6", if not taller, against my mother's 5'6" frame. I guess right around age sixteen or so, he began *smelling himself*, as the older folks would say.

Mama told him to do something, and he touted, "I'm not doing a damn thing."

Dray and I couldn't believe it. We ran for cover at the same time under the dining room table.

She collared Tony, flipped him over her back, and put her foot across his neck. How foolish! He knew she was a black belt in judo. Mama put her foot right across his larynx as Tony was trying to say something.

The more he tried to talk, the more she said, "I can't hear you, son. What's that you're saying?"

The whole situation was over in a matter of seconds.

Mama finally let him off the floor and told him to do what she said in the first place. That resolved him ever talking to her like that again. Unfortunately, there were many other challenges.

I clearly recall my mom nailing Tony's bedroom windows shut to keep him out of trouble because he would sneak out at night. My brother was addicted to the streets and simply found a hammer to remove the nails.

Late one night, the phone rang and it was Ms. Fran. There was something about my brother jumping through her front door because someone was shooting at him. Mama insisted that Tony was in his bedroom.

Something was said that made her take the cordless phone to Tony's bedroom and look for herself.

I heard my mom say, "Fran, he's in his bed."

Ms. Fran must have told her to pull the covers back. To her surprise, Tony had taken some pillows and formed them in the shape of his body in the same position he usually slept.

My mother's only response was "Tell him I said, 'Get home now,'" only her words weren't quite that nice.

Scary right? Well it gets scarier.

All the lights were turned off as she sat and waited for my brother to come home. By this time, Dray had snuck into my bedroom, which was right next to Mama's, to see what was going to happen. It seemed like hours had passed when we finally heard a key unlocking the front door.

Tony quietly came into the house and made it just past my bedroom before Mama clicked her light on and demanded he come into her room.

Tony looked so scared I felt sorry for him.

At first, Mama was giving him a lecture.

In the meantime, Dray and I snuck into the living room so we could get a closer look through a crack in Mama's bedroom door. That's when it happened! She brought a gun from behind her back.

All I remember hearing was, "I'm tired and I'm not staying up another night waiting to get a call, telling me you're dead. I'd rather get it over with now," then she pointed the gun at him.

Tony immediately fell to his knees and began begging for his life.

We later came to find out, he was never in jeopardy of being hurt. The gun wasn't loaded. I just think Mama was so desperate that she implemented her own scared straight program.

I was the one who almost died that night. When we saw the gun, Dray knew I was about to scream. He cupped his hand around my mouth, not realizing he was also covering my nose. Dray dragged me back into the bedroom before letting go and whispering how much trouble we'd be in. I have no clue if Mama heard us or not. All I know is I was kicking and struggling, trying to get some air.

At this point, I'm sure you may be thinking the term *child abuse*. Don't be so quick to judge! It's all about perspective. Today, it would no doubt be termed as child abuse, but back then, it was called parenting.

Mama and every black parent around did what they felt was necessary to keep their sons and daughters safe. I'm not saying it was right, but it was what they knew.

Police brutality and prison were just as real as it is today. The rate of mass incarceration for males in many urban communities played a large role in the devastation of countless black families. That doesn't include the infestation of legal and illegal drugs, along with liquor stores on almost every corner.

These weren't the only challenges, but certainly some of the major ones that led to the destruction of entire communities. Intentionally leading us down a path we still haven't recovered from.

Yes! Mama's fears were very real. She had a tough time being a single mother because Daddy was an absent parent for a long time. Thank God for my uncle Bob who lived with us, and Grandpa, who lived in Birmingham, Alabama. My grandfather stood in the gap and tried to do financially what his son should have been doing. I'm sure Grandpa was greatly disappointed in my father and likely spoke his mind on the matter.

I don't know what changed, but at some point, Daddy decided to try and build a relationship with me and my brothers. Dray nor

Tony seemed that impressed, but I was excited and wanted to spend time with him.

My dad started showing up at birthday parties and even took us to Edgewater Park. Tony, Dray, and I got on the spinning floor drop. After the ride stopped, I was so sick that everything inside me came up. Dray thought it was hilarious and had a good laugh about it. Overall, we had a great time, and I still remember it to this day.

Some time later, my father came to pick us up and said there was somebody we needed to meet. Mama was standing in the doorway as we were leaving, and she didn't look happy. Thinking back, she must've known where he was taking us.

When we arrived, I saw a picture sitting on the mantle. I turned and said, "Where are we? Why do they have a picture of me?"

Daddy laughed and replied, "That's not you; it's your sister, Diane."

The confused look on my face spoke for itself. I was Mama's only daughter. He didn't know how to explain it and just said she's your half sister.

With a serious look, I stared at him and said, "How can I have a half-a-sister?"

Everybody burst out laughing. It was right at that point a girl came down the stairs, and I stood there with my mouth open. She was an older version of me. There's no telling how long we stayed there, but it felt odd having a sister we knew nothing about.

When Daddy took us back home, I couldn't wait to tell Mama about my *half-a-sister*. The expression on her face immediately let me know this was not a topic to be discussed. I never brought it up again. I later learned from Grandpa that my dad had an affair while he and Mama were married. My half-sister was the result of that affair.

How heartbreaking that must have been because she so desperately wanted a girl at the time this happened. Surprisingly, Mama never spoke negatively of my dad. She wanted us to form our own opinion about who he was. It seemed like I was the only one who wanted to form any type of meaningful attachment.

We had become really close. I could tell he loved me, but wondered why it took him so long to come around. We talked on the phone a lot, and he always seemed to laugh at my jokes.

Our father-daughter bond was getting stronger when out of nowhere, Daddy unexpectedly had a massive heart attack. After a few weeks, the doctors said he had recovered and would be discharged in a couple of days.

That didn't happen. Without warning, we received news he'd passed away. I was completely devastated and didn't know what to do with my emotions. That's when I first started journaling and writing poetry.

He had just become a part of our lives, and in the blink of an eye, was stripped away. Everybody kept telling me that God knows best, and my dad's death was *His* will.

What kind of God would do that to a child? That sounded a lot to me like God killed my daddy. Adults need to be careful about what they say to children and choose their words more wisely. This taught me a valuable lesson about words. They hurt and can be destructive.

Chapter 1

The Institutionalization of a Community

"Be quiet before Mama hears us! Wonder what happens with all that food she packs up every week?"

"Beats me," Tony said. "It probably gets taken to one of those food places."

"What food places? Dray asked.

"You know, where people go to get free food."

"Stop *playing*," I whispered. "Everybody got food."

"No they don't," Tony insisted.

Just then, my mother closed the pantry door, and we all ran upstairs, not knowing she could hear us.

"Tony!" Mama yelled from the basement door. "Didn't I tell you to keep an eye on your brother and sister?"

"Yes, ma'am," he responded.

"Then why did I hear running up the basement stairs?"

"I *don'* know."

"Boy, pronounce your words correctly and don't lie to me, talking about you don't know. Now I asked you a question. What were you doing?"

Before Tony could answer, Dray started crying and had diarrhea of the mouth.

"We snuck downstairs to see what you were *doin'*, I mean doing. I didn't *wanna* but Tony made me go and said if we got caught, we'd all get in trouble together."

"That's just like your brother," Mama said. "All of you come help me bring these bags upstairs."

We looked at each other puzzled, because she didn't really sound mad. We hurried downstairs to help. After getting all the bags upstairs into the kitchen, I must've looked curious because Mama decided to explain why she packed bags of food.

"God has blessed us to have everything we need and some of what we want. There are people right here on our block that don't have nearly as much to eat as we do. It's our responsibility to do what we can."

My curiosity outweighed any fear of asking questions. "How come people don't have enough to eat? Are some of them my friends? Why do we have to give *'em* our food? What if we run out because we gave all ours away?"

Mama laughed and reminded me to pronounce my words clearly. She tried her best to answer each question as I shot them out like there was no tomorrow.

Eventually, she warned all of us not to discuss this with our friends or anyone. It would be embarrassing, and children can be cruel.

Neither of us ever told any of our friends but talked about it amongst ourselves. We were old enough to understand how cruel children could be when other parents struggled to provide the basic necessities.

I didn't know it then, but later came to know it was called poverty, not understanding that my family was also poor. Everyone seemed so happy and families were surviving despite the conditions of extreme *poverty*.

There's that word, haunting cities and communities across the country. It subliminally teaches people to associate their self-worth with the value of a dollar or material things known to represent wealth. Clearly we need money to survive, but it's the love of money that's the root of all evil. Right?

Webster's Dictionary defines *poverty* as "the state of one who lacks a usual or socially acceptable amount of money or material possessions."

Wait a minute! You mean to tell me that an individual is not socially acceptable unless the person can demonstrate they deserve to be accepted! If that's not the core thought process that has caused the institutionalized thinking of communities across this country, I don't know what is.

Mama hated the word *poverty*. She said it was a state of mind designed to convince people they were less than.

"Baby," she would say, "Having *less than* doesn't mean that you are *less than*. No matter where you are in life or what your financial circumstances are, always maintain your dignity. I want you to remember that money is necessary to live, but never live for money. A wealthy man has many people that call him friend until his wealth is gone, and then many become few."

It took a long time before I really knew what this meant. Wow, for someone who had less than a high school education, she was the smartest woman I knew.

Don't get me wrong, being poor is real and defined differently, depending on what part of the world you live in. I've witnessed it in developing countries where access to clean water is scarce. Animals and people use the same water to bathe, cook, and wash clothes. Orphanages are widespread due to impoverished conditions.

Medical treatment is limited, and people are dying from simple diseases like malaria. In some areas, a lottery is drawn to determine which children will be lucky enough to attend school, while others are denied.

In the United States, we have an educational system that's available to every child. Although substandard in many communities, our children have a right to public education.

Does poverty exist? Absolutely! We were poor growing up, but it was a long time before I knew it. Our home was like the Kool Aid house. Mama purchased a vacant lot and fenced it in, along with a huge backyard. Our friends would come over to play horseshoes, volleyball, and other outdoor games.

The outside was nicely manicured, and the inside was immaculate. Mama and Uncle Bob faithfully took precautions to seal cracks around the house and used professional sprays to ward off unwanted guests.

My mom always made sure we had good transportation and there was always a cellar full of canned goods, very neatly organized. I don't ever recall the refrigerator being empty!

I was shocked when she explained that we were underprivileged. In my young mind, being poor meant you didn't have enough food to eat and no place to live. If you had a house, it was unclean with a bad odor, infested with roaches.

Boy, did I get schooled! Mama educated me on the difference between the circumstances of being impoverished, compared to having the mindset of poverty.

In many situations, having a mentality of inferiority had little to do with the lack of financial resources. It was simply a thought process embedded in black communities. We were socialized to believe it was the norm. All too frequently, this way of thinking was generational. Many people became content and comfortable, while others rose above their conditions and valued what little they had.

Mama would say, "I don't care if we live in a two-bedroom shack. If that's all we have, then you best believe we're going to treat it like a mansion."

When you live with a deprived outlook, it leads to a road going nowhere fast. This same thought process made street life appealing to many boys and girls in my neighborhood. This was despite parents' attempts to steer them in a different direction.

Decent *God-fearing* families were trying their best to raise children in a challenging environment. Regrettably, even some of the *good* kids eventually got caught up. They became focused on changing their financial status from poor to less poor by any means necessary. It often involved fast money, designed as a systematic roadmap to prison or the cemetery.

I'm not saying that all kids got caught up with this way of thinking, but a lot did. Some were fortunate enough to avoid this trap and set their sights on college, jobs, the military, and other positive paths.

Neighborhoods were being infested with drugs, prostitution, and gambling. More dollars were diverted from educational establishments and redirected into the system of incarceration.

The ones that found themselves behind the walls of lost freedom, if they were lucky, learned to survive. Some who were initially nonviolent offenders returned as angry men and women with a more hostile nature.

An institution that was supposed to be a correctional facility did very little to correct and often created more violent predators. There were also those perpetrators that were like wolves, cloaked in sheep's clothing. They never experienced the cold walls of prison, but in many instances, were more dangerous and vicious.

We were no longer safe. No longer safe! It seemed that was just an illusion. *We were never safe!*

Safety was simply a word that existed to bring comfort to the minds of individuals. The safest place for children was supposed to be in their homes. We believed like Dorothy in the Wizard of Oz, "There's no place like home, there's no place like home."

Warnings were constantly discussed about not talking to strangers and what to do if someone tried to approach, touch, or coerce a child.

We prayed at night before bed and in the morning when we woke, for safety and protection. Children listened to their parents and stayed away from all the *shady* people. But what about the *enemy within*?

The perpetrator that came without warning. Fathers, brothers, teachers, aunts, uncles, coaches, mothers, family friends, and clergy. What about those who were supposed to protect and do no harm but committed violent sexual acts? Men and women who secretly shattered lives of innocent children for generations to come! Unleashing a rage destined for self-destruction. Anger that only a miracle could redirect.

Too many boys and girls fall into this type of fury and never find their way out. Thank God, after many years, I did.

My community was not rare, and my voice speaks for many *who never told*. Child molestation is nothing new. We would like to believe it's a newer phenomenon, but it's been around since the beginning of time. It's been hidden in households and family secrets.

The difference between then and now is the exposure given to well-known public figures. They're speaking more openly about their own trauma.

I'm so thankful they're using a public platform to increase awareness. We must also find better ways to encourage children to disclose sexual abuse sooner rather than later. There must be intentional strategies to empower them to be brave. I'm sure there are thousands of children frozen with fear and just waiting for someone to trust with their pain.

In-Her Rage

Her storms move angrily and forcefully in the atmosphere,
Violent winds and sounds grow stronger as they draw near.
Her cries are like a hurricane, ripping through small towns,
Then a calm in the eye, before her fury comes down.
The thunder in her voice gushes through hurt and pain,
Powerful floods of betrayal and mistrust will remain.
Hide from her temper, pray it doesn't come uncaged,
Destruction is all around her, but there's purpose in-her rage.

Chapter 2

It's Midnight

Sometimes family is all you got! Good, bad, or indifferent. We look out for each other and try to maintain the safety of our most vulnerable members, children, and seniors. That was Aunt Sarah. Always trying to do what she thought was necessary to keep me safe.

Aunt Sarah lived with us before she died from cancer. Auntie was all about safety. She was Mama's sister and my favorite aunt. Most people thought she was mean and had a sincere fear of her. Not me! The one thing I knew was that she loved her family and would tackle a flea for trying to bite one of us.

It was understood that Auntie didn't play, even though I was really young. She and my uncle Bob were the two people my mother completely trusted. Either of them would have given their lives for us, flat out!

At some point, Aunt Sarah found the need to teach me how to protect myself.

"Come here, baby girl," Auntie called from her bedroom. "Let me show you something. I need you to pay close attention because this might save your life one day."

She unwrapped her hair and pulled something out.

"You see this?" she asked.

"Yes, ma'am," I responded.

"It's called a straight razor, and you can really do some damage with this."

I was shocked! Yes, that's right. The woman was packing a razor in her hair! The surprise was only momentary as my fascination and curiosity got the best of me. I wanted to learn how she did it.

Auntie didn't hesitate to teach me how to wrap one in my hair, but also warned that I could never tell anybody or use it unless absolutely necessary. I took her instructions to heart and never used it until it was definitely crucial. I never told anyone, not even after she died, until now.

Mama was also no joke. She was well-respected and like my aunt, feared by a lot of people, adults and children alike. However, she had a much friendlier disposition than Aunt Sarah. Don't let that fool you because Mama typically said what she meant and meant what she said, especially when it came to her children.

Trust me, it was quite confusing why some of our friends and their parents felt she was the best mother in the world. Various women trusted Mama with horrible secrets about abusive boyfriends or husbands. Many sought her advice on how to handle their situations. They never knew I could hear their conversations through my bedroom wall.

As for me, I thought she was too strict, which seemed mean at the time. Mama didn't allow me the freedom that other girls in my neighborhood had. She was far too overprotective.

Unfortunately, I came to know that Mama could not be protective enough. There was no doubt in my mind the world would have been a much worse place without her in it. There were always those who hid their true identity.

Hidden behind the mask of titles were offenders watching and waiting to gain the trust of unsuspecting families. Looking for opportunities to prey on innocent children. Most of them didn't look like monsters or creepy people lurking around. No! They were frequently trusted or well-respected people with the perfect presentation to worm their way into homes.

The other type of predators were those that didn't have to sneak in; they were already there. Often causing the type of trauma that many children may never survive.

It leads to the question: why don't children tell? It's because we were conditioned not to. Adults frequently used catchphrases to keep us in line. A couple of favorites were "what happens in this household, stays in this household" and "children were made to be seen, not heard."

Another expression included, "I brought you into this world, and I'll take you out." Just about every black child around knew this phrase and understood it meant trouble.

Tony certainly came face-to-face with this threat. Parents used it as a control mechanism whenever children got a little too big for their britches (pants). It was another way of saying, "I gave you life, and I can take it away." Sounds a little biblical to me.

These idioms were engrained in us from early childhood. Children were trained to listen and do as they were told. Hugging grandparents, aunts, uncles, cousins, friends and others was a must, even when it was clear that a child didn't want too.

If only parents and caregivers had realized. How could they have known? Parents tend to rear children in the manner they were raised. Far too often, individuals with titles were trusted not because they earned it, but simply because of their positions. This fact is still true today, but hopefully changing.

The church and educational systems were the foundation of our community. Teachers, family members, pastors, and others were almost automatically a trusted source. Don't misunderstand me. We need and deserve all the wonderful people provided to us.

My point is, a title doesn't make the man or woman. Many ill-intentioned people are cloaked with good deeds and appearance of sincerity. We must be more observant and vigilant over the safety of our children. We can't protect them from everything, as Mama so adamantly tried to do. We can reduce the risk of harm by arming ourselves and children with knowledge.

Dare to be that *overprotective* parent, sibling, relative, or friend, as it may be what saves a child's life or mental stability.

It was a pastor who tried to shatter my mind around the age of seven. Bill became a part of Mama's circle as an avid fisherman. It was one of her favorite pastime activities. Many Friday nights, we helped her and my uncle water the lawn. It was so fun because we got to stay up late and help collect bait (worms). My mom, Uncle Bob, and a number of other people would get up early Saturday morning and head to Wah-Poh Island or some other well-known fishing spot.

Sometimes we went fishing with them and loved showing off our poles. However, it was a long time before my brothers and I were introduced to Bill. We just knew he was a part of the fishing crew. This was likely because Mama was suspicious of people overall, and she never allowed men in our home.

Mama knew a lot of police officers and was very cautious. During a phone conversation, I overheard her and a friend talking about running all kinds of criminal background checks on Bill. They must have come back clear because she slowly began allowing him to spend time at our home.

At some point, we started visiting Bill's church, which I didn't like. From a child's perspective, there were a lot of older people who couldn't sing and dressed funny. It was obvious Mama didn't like being there either. I couldn't figure out why she kept visiting a place she really didn't enjoy. I dared not ask for risk of getting in trouble. It turned out all I had to do was wait because our attendance was short-lived, but Bill kept coming around.

Mama and Uncle Bob were always very watchful whenever Bill or anyone outside our household came over. Especially when it came to me and my two younger cousins, Niecy and Margaret. He apparently convinced them of his trustworthiness because he started coming over more frequently.

I don't quite remember everything, but there was a short period of time (seemed like months) when my uncle, aunt (his wife), and cousins left town. That's when Mama became really sick and was on a lot of strong medication. It kept her tired and drowsy.

She didn't have much of a support system. By this time my aunt Sarah was dead. Grandpa was blind and lived in Alabama, Uncle Bob was gone, and Aunt Mary was not yet in the picture.

My mother had to trust somebody, so she felt it was safe to trust Bill. Mama was in a lot of pain and her medication made her sleepy a lot. She needed someone to help supervise my brothers and I. That's when Bill readily availed himself.

He was a funny guy with removable teeth that made us laugh. It was hilarious whenever he took them out of his mouth with his tongue then quickly put them back in. That was Bill's way of bonding with us. Trying to gain our trust. Dray and Tony never liked him, but I was more impressionable.

As days went by, Mama seemed to grow more tired, and I started becoming afraid. It seemed she was always in pain like Aunt Sarah used to be. It must have concerned Mama too.

One particular night, I heard her and Bill talking in the living room. She asked him to do something she'd never done before.

"Bill," Mama said, "do you mind staying in the guest room tonight and keeping an eye on the kids while I get some sleep?" She knew we could be really mischievous without proper supervision.

"Of course I wouldn't mind," he responded.

"Thank you, that would be a big help."

Mama didn't go into her room right away. She helped me get ready for bed while Bill assisted my brothers under her watchful eyes. They made sure we ate and got to bed at a decent time.

Mama kissed me and my brother's goodnight, turned off the bedroom lights, and I fell fast asleep staring at my night light. It was a peaceful sleep until I woke up to the touch of someone's hand. I rubbed the sleep from my eyes and could clearly see it was Bill.

Before any words were spoken, he put one finger to his lips and said, "Shhh, everybody's sleep."

I was confused but not really afraid. At least not yet. He leaned down and kissed me on one cheek and then the other. He did this a few times, so I thought it was a game like Mama and I sometimes played at bedtime. Before long, Bill kissed me on my lips. I was stunned but curious. At first, it was small pecks, then his breathing got heavier and the kisses became stronger. More wet! My body tensed as I began to get scared.

Bill must have sensed my fear because he went back to gentle kisses. I could feel him touching me up and down before easing his hands into my pajama pants. I became terrified, couldn't move, but for some reason, I didn't scream.

Mama always told me nobody is supposed to touch me down there. My mind was saying tell him to stop. The right thing to do was scream. Yell help! Say no! The words just wouldn't come out of my mouth. Maybe it was because I was frozen with fear. Maybe in my young mind, I knew my mother or uncle would go to prison for killing him, and it would be my fault. Especially since I always heard my family talking about what they would do if anybody ever hurt one of us.

It was as if Bill read my thoughts and said, "If you tell your mom or uncle, they will kill me. You don't want them to go to prison, do you? If they go to prison, you and your brothers will go into foster care with strangers. They do bad things to kids."

The words are still fresh in my mind today. It was the beginning of him grooming me, a little girl.

Mama was sick for what seemed to be forever. I'm sure it was a short period of time, but as a child, it seemed like forever. Nonetheless, there were many more nights that Bill came into my bedroom. Each time, he was more daring and demonstrated more of what he called *love*. Eventually I was made to perform all kinds of adult acts. Oddly enough, he never penetrated me. Bill knew my mother paid close attention to any signs of physical trauma. He had enough sense not to risk causing injury, at least not physically.

Bill was supposed to represent God, but instead he used his title as a pastor to gain trust and cause harm. Unfortunately, some of us learned the hard way that a title doesn't make the person. It was just a mask that he used to hide his real identity.

My self-esteem and self-confidence were shattered for a time. When I looked into the mirror, the only thing that looked back at me was an ugly girl. I certainly didn't feel *fearfully and wonderfully made*. They were just words in a book that I didn't really understand any-way. Where was this God everyone talked about that was a protector?

Eventually, I learned how to wear a mask of my own. It was a mask of smiles that kept me hidden when hurt or pain invaded my space. Inside I was raging. I was dangerous. My spirit was broken, and the aftermath of sexual trauma lasted long after the abuse stopped.

Ultimately, Mama recovered from her sickness and became more alert. Uncle Bob returned home, and Bill no longer had opportunity. I don't think I ever demonstrated any of the typical signs of sexual abuse like reverting back to wetting the bed or anything. However, I became unusually clingy to my uncle. Everyone probably associated this with me missing him so much.

I later rationalized in my mind, as much as a little girl could, that Bill didn't really hurt me. I knew it was wrong! I just didn't have the intellectual capacity at the time to understand it was still rape.

The last thing I recall about Bill was my mother going to the grocery store and leaving him in charge of me and my brothers. My oldest brother was very hyperactive and refused to listen.

"Sit down and stop all that running around," Bill yelled.

Tony was a little older now and retorted, "You ain't my daddy, and you can't tell me what to do."

It made Bill mad, and without warning, he snatched Tony by the arm and slapped him.

All at once, Tony, Dray, and I bum-rushed Bill and begin kicking, biting, and punching. I wanted to use the razor blade hidden in my hair but quickly remembered my aunt's words and decided not to.

I was screaming, "Let him go, you pervert."

Dray was on one leg, I was on the other, and Tony was punching until Bill lost his grip on him. He ended up falling off balance and went tumbling down. It was like David and Goliath except there were three stones that brought the giant down. He seemed surprised that we attacked him.

What Bill didn't know was that we were always told if one of us gets into a fight, we all better fight. Even if it meant getting beat down.

After it was over, the three of us got scared because we didn't know what Mama's reaction would be. Neither of us had ever fought an adult before. But then again, we never had too.

When my mother returned home, you could hear an ant walk across the carpet. We were sitting quietly, watching TV and didn't even acknowledge her when she walked through the door. Bill was sitting in a corner chair, probably just as scared as we were. Something inside Mama, perhaps maternal instincts, must have sensed something horribly wrong. Shortly after that, the monster was gone, and Mama never brought anyone else into our home to take charge of us.

I could be *safe* again. That is until my body began filling out in places I didn't like earlier than expected. My breast were getting larger, my hips wider, and my rear bigger. In an effort not to draw attention to myself, I wore baggy jeans and T-shirts.

I didn't feel attractive, was the tallest girl in my class, and had grown comfortable with my ugly duckling complex. Unfortunately, this didn't stop the next predator from waiting for the perfect opportunity to make his move.

It's Midnight

Innocence crushed, thrust against a wall. Silently
I cried, with no words spoken at all.
A mask that became as black as the night. I feared
shadows of darkness, where is the light?
Rage fueled my purpose and obeyed my every command. Anger
concealed with a thousand smiles, wanting to take a stand.
Who do you think you are, taking what doesn't belong to you?
My mind is a collage of confusion, not knowing what to do.
You boasted about your title, but it made not the man.
My spirit is only fractured and will soon become whole again.
Daybreak will come soon, and I'll say goodbye to midnight.
Everything you meant for wrong, will one day be made right.
But for now, it's midnight, and a burden of terror I must bear.
A season of virtue lost, with the guilt of shame and despair.
Where is beauty's mirror, will she find me in the sunlight? Soon
the warmth of her reflection will shine through my midnight.

Chapter 3

Enough

It was a hot summer day, and all the kids were given permission to go to the neighborhood grocery and candy store. I was about ten years old. Mama would only allow me to go if my brothers escorted me.

There was supposed to be safety in numbers so several of us cut through the alley and vacant lots. I caught a glimpse of Rocky out the corner of my eyes as we ran past where he was standing. He was watching as we barreled toward the store.

My brothers, who usually stuck to me like glue, ran ahead to beat the other kids getting to the store. That's when I heard someone calling my name. He was yelling that my mom wanted me to come back home.

"It was too good to be true. She never lets me go anywhere," I mumbled.

There was no doubt that she had changed her mind about letting me go to the store. I was screaming to the top of my lungs for my brothers to turn around, but there was too much laughing and noise. It was impossible for them to hear me.

As I headed back home, pouting, Rocky timed it perfectly. He grabbed my arm, put his hand across my mouth, dragged me into his filthy garage and slammed the door shut. I was thrown into the back seat of an old car that had no doors.

The horrible stench of his body and the vehicle remain in my memory.

Somehow Rocky had already unzipped his pants, and they were slightly down below his hips. I was terrified at what he was about to do. Panic almost immobilized me. He was grabbing at my pants trying to unfasten them. I began kicking and fighting like my life depended on it. Becoming exhausted, my mind started racing as I tried to think about what to do.

All that came to mind was, "God, help me. Why are you letting this happen again?"

Suddenly a voice said, "Fight harder."

I started swinging with all my might, trying to scream, but Rocky had his hand over my mouth. It was difficult to breathe, and he used all the weight of his body to pin me down.

It felt like I was being smothered to death as my body began giving up when the voice said, "Now you can use it."

At first, my mind raced to remember what *it* was. Then my aunt's instructions came flooding back. "Never use *it* unless absolutely necessary."

Somehow, I managed to free one of my arms, which had become pinned under Rocky's body. I quickly located the razor tucked in my hair. Without thinking about cutting myself, I grabbed whatever piece was sticking out and started swinging. Fear caused me to strike out in every direction. Apparently it worked because Rocky started screaming and cursing. The more he screamed, the more I swung until he raised up enough for me to break free.

While running out of the garage as quickly as possible, I yelled, "I'm telling my uncle, and he's going to kill you. I'm telling everybody!

I ran all the way home, across my backyard, through the backdoor of our house, up the backstairs to tell my uncle. Something stopped me dead in my tracks. Bill's voice was loud in my ear. "If you tell, you know your mom and uncle will kill me. They'll go to prison."

Robotically, my body turned and retreated to the basement, crying, shaking, and scared. After a few minutes, I snuck upstairs and went into my bedroom. Mama was on the phone and never heard me come in, so when my brothers ran past her bedroom door, she assumed I was with them.

They looked scared and relieved because they realized I had never made it to the store.

"What happened to you?" Tony whispered. "Did you tell Mama we left you?"

I started crying and responded, "No, but you left me behind. Mama told you never to let me out of your sight."

After my brothers started profusely apologizing, I promised not to tell.

Dray was more observant and noticed dry tears on my face.

"Are you okay?" he asked. "Why were you crying?"

"Because *y'all* left me." I asked him again, "Why did you leave me? I was scared!"

Right then the words almost came out my mouth about Rocky, but it was a secret they would never agree to keep. I felt safe now and hugged my brothers real tight. I told them they'd better never leave me like that again and they never did.

A few days later, I went outside with my brothers, attempting to act normal. I stuck really close to them. Wherever they went, little sis was right on their heels.

Tony and Dray were engaged in horseplay but constantly checked to make sure they weren't too far ahead.

Eventually, the moment I dreaded happened. We walked in the direction of Rocky's house, where his little brother (Shorty), best friend (Puff) and grandfather (Mr. Tom) were sitting on the porch. Just as we were about to walk pass, Shorty spotted me. He started telling their grandfather about what happened. Shorty couldn't pronounce words clearly, and his grandfather was half deaf, so it was hard to understand what he was saying.

My brothers were busy goofing off and not paying any attention to their conversation, but I clearly heard what was being said. Puff was sitting on the porch and understood as well.

Puff immediately shut Shorty down then looked at me with complete fear and shook his head no. I knew what he was silently saying as his head just kept nonverbally saying, "No, they'll kill him."

That moment is when I learned Shorty saw Rocky pull me into the garage and witnessed the whole ordeal. He knew his brother was trying to rape me and never ran to get help. How could anyone just stand there and listen to the violent assault that was occurring?

From that point forward, I hated Shorty and always found myself in some kind of altercation with him. What's worse is Puff, an adult, knew exactly what happened. He was more interested in protecting his friend than my traumatic experience.

Once again, I never told. The next morning, there was less fear and more anger. Not just toward Rocky but every man that destroyed innocence like him and Bill.

I wanted so desperately to tell my mom but was more grateful for the voice that gave me instruction.

Say what you will about spirits, but an angel was with me that day. I believed it was the voice of my aunt Sarah at the time but would later come to believe it was something more powerful.

Who can understand why God delivered me in that moment! All I know is the voice was real.

The next time I saw Rocky, he looked like a deer in headlights. Scared! I took advantage of the situation. Always taunting him with the threat of telling. As far as he was concerned, at least one other person knew, just in case he ever thought about trying to hurt me again.

On that day, empowerment became a thing. On that day, vows became real to never let anyone try to hurt me like that again. On that day, anger gave me purpose. On that day, I promised to protect any of my friends that were being sexually violated or physically assaulted. On that day, I had enough.

Enough

Enough! No more will the reach of your hand harm me. I was born of my mother, but more importantly, I am my Father's child. Born the child of a King, conditioned to be strong and withstand the ferocious winds and storms that come my way.

Enough! Your sickness has been revealed and secrets are no longer safe. You can't destroy who I was born to be. You can't take my self-identification, and I refuse to give it to you.

Enough! I won't be a slave to fear because of you. I won't stand idly by and watch you destroy other lives with your deceit. You thought your actions conquered my spirit and weakened my mind. But the chains that were intended to shackle, freed an eagle destined to soar. *Enough!*

Chapter 4

Do you hear me?

I was ashamed of the secrets tucked deep down inside of me. Hiding feelings of ugliness and low self-worth. Surely, no one else could possibly have such horrible people in their lives. My thoughts on this changed when I met a new friend.

Charisma was an only child being raised by her aunt and uncle, Joe and Rosie Starky, who had no children of their own. Her mother died during childbirth and she never knew her father.

The Starky's did pretty good financially. They lived in a beautiful suburban home and provided Charisma with the best of everything. She attended the most prestigious schools and dressed in nothing but the finest designer apparel. Everyone envied her because she was living the life that most kids could only dream of.

We became really good friends after getting involved in an afro-centric performing arts program. Our love for singing, dancing, and acting allowed us to have a common bond. It was great! I was laughing again, not just smiling. It was wonderful learning more about our heritage, ancestors and the history of black people in Africa and America.

Charisma and I spent a lot of time together. Her aunt was very protective of her, but liked and trusted Mama. In due time, she was allowed to start coming to our house. I thought Charisma wouldn't be comfortable because our home wasn't nearly as lavish as she described hers. It was amazing to see how much she loved being there. We always got sad when it came time for her to go home.

We were like two peas in a pod. Never seeing one of us without the other. I recall one day while rehearsing, something in the play must have triggered Charisma. She started crying.

My first thought went straight to someone bullying her. I immediately switched to fight mode and wanted to know who. I was going to protect Charisma the same way my brothers were taught to protect me.

Nothing could have prepared my mind for what she finally shared. At first, there was pure shock, then a familiar rage began surfacing. It was more powerful than ever before. I didn't want to feel the anger and tried to fight it. What she revealed next was worse than anything I had ever been exposed to.

My friend was definitely being bullied in the worst kind of way. Uncle Joe was supposed to love and protect. Instead he repeatedly and violently raped his niece every opportunity he got. Waiting for his wife to fall sound asleep.

Aunt Rosie was a pretty sound sleeper. Her husband knew that nothing short of an earthquake would wake her up. He transformed Charisma's place of safety into a place of horror. Good old uncle brutalized her body like a stranger on the street. She had been suffering through these painful encounters for many years.

I felt helpless and couldn't understand how a man could be so cruel to anyone, let alone his own niece. Why didn't she tell? Why didn't I?

I was too little to fight a grown man her uncle's size, so in my young mind, a plan was devised to keep her safe. We convinced her aunt to allow Charisma to spend weekends at my house. It worked for a while until Uncle Joe started complaining about Charisma being gone so much. What he was really complaining about was not having as much access to my friend.

Guilt started overcoming me as thoughts about how lucky I was crossed my mind. Bill or Rocky didn't get the chance to hurt me the way Charisma was being hurt.

We talked about the abuse by Bill and how Rocky got sliced up for trying to rape me. My ordeal was nothing like what she was going through.

Sadly, I looked at her and said, "They didn't hurt me here (pointing between my legs), but they hurt me here (pointing at my head)."

Unfortunately, Charisma was being hurt in both places. We cried and bonded over something so painful. Two young girls keeping unspeakable secrets. But then again, we were unintentionally conditioned to keep silent.

The rage inside continued to grow. It scared me as I began having what came to be known as homicidal thoughts.

I wanted to protect my friend and tell the women in our lives about the men they trusted. There was a desire to divulge but knew I couldn't. Charisma carried a different burden than me. I knew my family would trust my word and feared the threat of any of them going to prison. My friend was terrified of not being believed. She was conditioned to think that no one would take her word over his. He would make it appear as if she was a spoiled little liar.

"I've given you everything," her uncle stated. "I'm a well-respected person in this community and no one would ever believe you."

What kind of woman wouldn't see the signs of such a sick person? Why didn't Charisma's aunt recognize that something was wrong in her home? Why didn't Mama?

These are great questions. Regrettably, there aren't always clear signs of abuse. Also, most individuals who sexually abuse children don't walk around advertising themselves. They look like everyday people who are skilled at learning how to access vulnerable families and children.

It's a mistake to believe that a background check alone makes a person safe to be around young kids or other at-risk populations. Many perpetrators have never been exposed to the criminal justice system.

Mama was very cautious when it came to Bill, and Uncle Joe never had a criminal record. Both were trusted members of the community. They wore a mask that portrayed themselves in a positive light. Neither cared about the aftermath their actions would leave behind.

The extent of Charisma's trauma was extremely difficult to reverse. It led to years of substance abuse, mental health challenges and other self-destructive behaviors.

Our friendship slowly began to fade as she was unable to overcome the trauma of her abuse. I'm sure she grew into a young woman who was angry, confused, and untrusting. Looking for love in all the wrong places. I can only imagine that she was in and out of therapy, trying to fix what was broken. Trying to gather shattered little pieces of innocence lost.

As I reflect on my own trauma, I'm sure Charisma experienced many failed relationships. Each one building on the pain of previous ones. Always wanting to believe that the next one will be better.

How many more children must become broken before the sickness of this world is put to rest? What causes the mind of a person to be so fragmented that it leads them down a path of pure evil?

Surely, Charisma and I must have been two of the unluckiest children in the world. No one else could possibly have experienced such hurt. No one else would ever keep quiet about the monsters in their life. At least that's what I thought until I met Shack and his two brothers, Don and Pete.

Do You Hear Me?

Can you end this nightmare and clear my mind?
Do you hear me calling, what peace can I find?
I pray and I pray, lifting my voice up to you,
I say, "Father help me, I don't know what to do."
I carry this anger that's killing me inside,
I'm tired of running and there's nowhere to hide.
The storm keeps brewing, and the wind is high
Babies dying, people lying, somebody just tell me why.
My spirit says surrender, but my flesh won't obey,

Seems the battle inside gets stronger every day.
Father, do you hear me, please rescue me from it all,
Do you hear my voice, my cry, my plea when I call?
These circumstances before me are all such a mess.
Where is my calm? When can my mind be at rest?

Chapter 5

Be Courageous

Around the age of fifteen I met Shack at a two-week camp one summer where my mom allowed me and my brothers to go. Amazingly, we didn't live too far from each other and became really good friends. Shack, Don, and Pete lived in a two-parent household with their mother and father, Mr. and Mrs. Peper. That later changed when his parents separated and divorced.

Shack was the oldest, and like my brothers, was responsible for watching over his younger siblings. It was apparent he loved them, but they seemed very uncomfortable showing any type of affection or physical contact.

His dad worked and was never around anymore. However, when he was at home, there was always heavy drinking, screaming, and hitting. Mr. Peper mostly hit his mom but would turn on him if he tried to help.

There was a situation where Mr. Peper beat his mother so bad she ended up in the hospital for three weeks. During that time, Mr. Peper would take his frustrations out on the three brothers. Shack would take the brunt of his father's abuse, trying to protect his siblings.

I really respected Shack for his toughness and willingness to look out for his brothers, even at the risk of being harmed himself. It reminded me of my brothers.

As time went on, we were inseparable. He became one of my closest friends. We could talk about anything, and it would never make its way back to us through the grapevine. Finally, a male I could completely trust, and he trusted me. We had the type of brotherly-sisterly attachment that I'd never experienced before outside of my own brothers.

Even though we attended different schools, it didn't break our bond. There was a closeness that even Mama didn't seem concerned about. She never discouraged the relationship and liked Shack's protectiveness of his brothers and me. I became really comfortable talking to him about everything.

I eventually shared my experience about Bill and Rocky. How it messed me up mentally, but at the same time, made me stronger.

"They tried to break me," I said to Shack as he intensely listened. "Bill used his position to gain my family's trust. As soon as Mama got sick, he took full advantage of the opportunity. Bill made me do things that little kids should never have to go through."

Shack sat quietly with his arm around my shoulder until I finished describing the painful experience.

He then began to share the impact of his parent's divorce. It was hard on all the brothers but seemed harder on him. Like many children, he really loved his dad despite his faults.

I always felt like there was more he wanted to tell me and for whatever reason, just couldn't. I never asked and figured he would tell when the time was right.

For now, Shack was concerned about his mother getting back into the workforce. She had always been a stay-at-home mom and was really nervous about other people watching her children. Even though Shack was in high school, she wanted him and his brothers to have adult supervision.

Since no parent can be with their children 24–7, Mrs. Peper had to trust someone, right? So why not trust a family member. That's exactly what she did. Who would be concerned about leaving their sons in the hands of their own brother? This is someone Mrs. Peper grew up with and had known all her life. Besides, after her brother's release, he always helped out with the kids.

Uncle Big was incarcerated some years ago for drug trafficking but was paroled early when the boys were really young. Shack never seemed to like his uncle much; however, he was respectful and careful not to talk back.

Uncle Big seemed to be a woman's man and boasted about the number of women he had. They didn't seem to mind that he was an ex-con who'd spent a number of years in prison. As a matter of fact, it appeared to be a chick magnet.

Shack was always turned off by the way his uncle used women. He seemed to have a bitter disposition when it came to this particular family member.

One day, while talking, I mentioned his uncle. Shack's demeanor visibly changed. He did something I'd never seen him do before. Out of the blue, tears started streaming down his face, and his fists were clenched.

I knew immediately there was a problem and readied myself to have his back, whatever it was.

My buddy was a pretty tough kid, so to see him cry made me tear up. I never asked what was wrong, but just grabbed his hand. It seemed like we were there for hours.

After he wiped his face and calmed down, Shack started talking about school stuff at first. Afterwards, he moved into life before and after his parent's divorce. As I listened, there was only one emotion. No tears, no fear, no hurt, just pure rage.

Somewhere along the way, Uncle Big became involved in a brutal lifestyle where he developed a desire for little boys. There were plenty of men he could have been with. Why assault innocent children that he claimed to *love* so much?

Maybe it was due to easy access, or maybe not. Either way, his actions would reach deep into the mental stability of this family for years to come.

As Shack continued to describe the details of sexual abuse expanding over years, I grew more and more angry.

Why did people our parents trusted, keep hurting us? Why couldn't other people see how sick these individuals were? *Why? Why? Why*, Lord, do you keep putting people in my path? I have no power to help them because I can't even help myself.

Shack and his brothers were forced to do disgusting acts with each other. I don't know when it started. Based on what he was sharing, it had never stopped for his younger brothers, as he had just discovered.

That explained why the brother's ability to naturally interact with each other was severely damaged.

Uncle Big convincingly put Shack and his brothers in a state of fear, threatening to kill them and their mother (his sister) if they ever told. So like myself and others, the brothers were conditioned not to tell.

Uncle Big continued coming around as if everything was normal while Shack and his brothers lived in complete terror.

We were just kids! Life should have been fun. This wasn't fair and it was time to do something about it. I was always aware that Mama kept multiple weapons in the house.

Children are very observant!

It was going to be my job to keep them safe from now on. Out of nowhere, I asked if he wanted his uncle gone. Shack didn't appear to be surprised. That's because he was already thinking about doing something himself.

It was completely quiet as he contemplated my question. Finally, the silence was broken when he said "Yeah, let's do this."

Jokingly, we talked about how Uncle Big wouldn't be around to hurt any other children. Every day Shack would make funny faces to demonstrate how his uncle would look after he was dead.

There were multiple conversations about what we wanted to do and how. At first, I thought it was just us blowing off some steam, but the more we talked, the more real it felt.

During our last discussion, I asked Shack if he was scared. He said, "Like a pig going to slaughter." It made me laugh, but I was afraid too.

We were both good kids and had never gotten into any serious trouble, let alone talking about harming someone.

Fear was trying to take the place of my anger. I refused to let that happen. We committed to stopping the violent assaults and that was all there was to it. Who did these people think they were? Folks using authority to treat children like their own personal property to do with as they will! It *ain't goin'* down like that!

The plan was to wait until Shack's high school homecoming dance, sneak out, and return before anybody noticed. It wouldn't be that hard since Uncle Big only lived two blocks from the school.

There was just one problem: Mama would never let me go anywhere without my brothers. I knew Dray was a homebody and wouldn't want to go unless Mama made him. It would be a lot easier to ditch Tony because he was always the life of the party.

I was concerned she wouldn't allow me to go to the dance. After pleading my case, Mama agreed to let Tony take me. Shack was a boy, so he didn't have any problems with getting permission from his mom.

We had three weeks before our lives would change forever. My unconscious mind was so bothered that I started having repeated nightmares. The dreams were always very similar in nature.

Shack and I rang the doorbell at his Uncle's place. He would invite us in to sit and watch TV with him. Each time, we stepped into the house but declined to have a seat and made up an excuse for stopping by. Just as we were turning to leave, four men broke into the house and ordered us to get on the sofa next to Uncle Big. One of them had a shot gun, and the other three had what appeared to be Semi-automatic weapons.

I would force myself to wake up before the outcome was revealed from fear of what I'd see. After the last dream, I talked with Shack and told him about all the nightmares.

"What do you think it means?" he asked.

I responded, "I'm not sure but everything was so clear, and I remember every detail. I think it's a warning for us. If we go, something bad is going to happen."

Shack looked like he was trying to make sense of it all, and chose to believe me. Together we decided to abandon our stupid plans to do something disastrous. Following through would've had lifelong consequences.

I caution parents! Don't assume life's influences can't lead your kids astray because you're a *good* parent.

Shack and I still went to his homecoming dance and had a ball. Dancing, laughing, and just having some good old-fashioned fun.

That night, Tony watched me like a hawk. He seemed to pay attention to my every move. Even while on the dance floor, he never forgot to glance around to see exactly where I was. It was probably his way of keeping the promise that he and Dray made to never leave me again. It didn't bother me because there was nothing to hide anymore.

After the dance, I kept thinking how foolish it was for us to even consider what we were contemplating. My dream also kept coming back to the forefront of my mind and how real it felt. Something was coming. I just didn't know when.

A while after the homecoming dance, I got a phone call from my friend. I could hardly understand him. He was talking fifty miles a minute. Once Shack calmed down, I was not stunned by what was said.

Uncle Big was dead. Somebody broke into his house and shot him. The police stated it appeared he was killed with some type of shotgun.

Admittedly, it was difficult to understand my emotional state of mind. Mostly because there was very little reaction. The coldness I felt about someone being killed bothered me. Before I could say anything, Shack brought up my dream.

He asked, "How did you know?"

My response was, "I don't know." It would be quite a while before things were made clear.

Nonetheless, I was extremely happy we didn't go to his uncle's house that night or any time thereafter. I also couldn't help being relieved that Shack's brothers would no longer have to be afraid in their own home anymore.

This would hopefully allow him and his brothers an opportunity to heal. It wasn't going to be easy, and would probably take a long time before they could show any type of natural affection toward each other.

Shack and I remained friends for what seemed like a long period of time. Unfortunately, he and his family moved out of state. We lost contact after a while, but I often wonder how things turned out for them.

As for me, I had my own demons to battle but was determined not to let them win.

Be Courageous

A lion's courageous roar is a frightening sound. Don't give into the fear, let courage embrace you. Let it engulf your environment. The courage of a person is knowing when to stand their ground. Don't give into defeat. Don't give up on the strength of courage. Fight with all your might. Get angry and fight! Eradicate the dark mind that dare to bring harm to the innocent. Fight…fight…fight!

Run now! Run toward your destiny and not away. Run forward in your purpose! Don't surrender your passion. Let the fire burning inside keep you fueled. Who told you that your voice didn't matter? Who told you not to be bold? Speak now! I want to hear your voice. It's too quiet. Where is the noise of your outpouring? Be courageous!

Chapter 6

Splintered Pieces

The trauma of childhood sexual abuse frequently shapes the way we build relationships with others. Particularly when it comes to intimate connections.

Some of us attach ourselves to people who fill a void of innocence lost. Others may search for a sense of belonging, leading us to look for love in all the wrong places. That was me! Chasing after a princess fantasy, even when it hurt.

Trust, love and betrayal were one in the same. They were a triangle of codependent habits. This became more evident in my relationship with Brad. He became what no individual should ever be. My everything!

It was unbelievable! Some really nice-looking brothers moved into the neighborhood. Of course, all the girls were anxious to find out more about them. Including me!

My chances were slim to none. I wasn't the most attractive person in the world and carried myself as such. A good description would be *tomboy*. Perhaps this was a way for me to ward off unwanted attention as my body continued to develop in undesirable areas.

Most of the girls were very pretty and had the perfect outward appearance that boys liked. It didn't stop me from looking and wishing I could call one of them my boyfriend.

I specifically had my eyes on the oldest tall, dark, and gorgeous brother, Brad. It didn't matter because my mother would never allow me to date. Especially not him because he was a few years older. I figured looking was harmless as long as no one caught me.

Curiosity led to a little snooping. I found out that their mother, Ms. Loar, faithfully took them to church. It seemed like every evening and all day on Sundays.

My mind immediately went to, *the preacher* must be a liar. Since pastors weren't my favorite people, I just knew he was getting rich off his membership. Convincing them to be in church every day, giving their tithes and offerings or they'll go to hell.

I couldn't see any purpose in such foolishness and felt bad for the whole family. If it took going to church every day to be saved, my soul would be going to hell. Sunday was enough for me.

The family's attendance at church didn't stop my infatuation with Brad. There was a desire to find out more about them. That's when the opportunity presented itself.

One day, I was in my backyard and decided to climb the big cherry tree we had. One of Brad's brother's, Foster, was walking by and saw me climbing the tree. He could see into my backyard from the lot next to our house that Mama bought and fenced in.

Foster immediately yelled out, "Hey, would it be okay if I come into your yard?"

My response was "Sure, if you want to risk getting shot by my mom or uncle."

There was a brief pause before he jumped the fence. Foster was a typical boy and wanted to demonstrate how much faster he was at climbing than me.

Yeah, right! I dusted him.

We laughed really hard and decided to be friends. My mother must have been okay with it because she never ran him off. Maybe because I didn't show any schoolgirl crush.

After a while, Foster and I started talking about the Bible from time to time. He invited me to their church. It was intriguing how much he seemed to know, but not enough to be in nobody's church all day and night.

47

I told Foster his pastor was probably a liar and taking all his mom's money. We laughed and I agreed to ask my mother so we could move on to something else. Foster wouldn't let it go though. At least not until I made a promise to inquire.

My word was not bond. Whenever Foster came around, he would remind me to ask Mama about going to church. Selective memory always kicked in. His persistence caused me to give in about a year later. In my heart, I knew Mama would never agree to it, especially with me being the only girl.

Can you believe the one time I wanted her to say no she said, "Let me speak with Ms. Loar first." Go figure!

By this time, my mother was allowing me to attend church with some of my other neighbors so I knew what to expect. I liked the music and got a kick out of watching people jumping around. Once the music was over, I didn't want to hear anything the pastor had to say. Even when the adults would tell me to pay attention, I pretended to listen and frequently found myself daydreaming about Brad.

Mama was apparently satisfied after her conversation with Ms. Loar. She gave approval for me to attend their church. I couldn't contain my excitement, but it had nothing to do with trying to learn about the Bible. At the time, it was just an opportunity to finally talk to Brad.

When the day arrived, Mama helped me pick out a nice outfit to wear. She insisted that early morning mass at our church came first. I was fine with that. My church was Catholic and usually only lasted about an hour. That was plenty of time.

After service was over, I came home, changed into my *fancy* clothes and walked to church with Brad and his family. I stuck close to Ms. Loar as Mama instructed, but kept a close eye on Brad. He was dressed in a black suit and looked really nice. I tried my best not to stare and be polite whenever he engaged me in conversation.

When we got to the church, there was great disappointment and some jealousy. Brad had a girlfriend who was acting all holier-than-thou. My mind immediately went to, *it's time to go home*.

Once church started it seemed like we were there forever.

Finally, service ended, and it was time to go home. At least that's what I thought before the pastor announced the second service would start at three thirty. He wanted everyone to stay for something to eat. It was tempting as the smell of fried chicken filled the air. It probably would have been good, but the only thought that came to my mind was, *I ain't stayin' here for no second service.*

Foster must have read my thoughts. He proceeded to tell Ms. Loar not to forget my mom was expecting me home by a certain time. Foster offered to walk me home. Initially, Ms. Loar said yes but for some reason changed her mind and told Brad to walk me home.

You've got to be kidding me! This was my chance to talk to Brad alone. I was initially very hesitant and uncomfortable because you never know what people are capable of. The fear quickly past when Brad's girlfriend became visibly upset.

If he tried something, on our way home, my blade was just a hair strand away. I was always on guard but really didn't feel threatened by my new crush.

My instincts were right! Brad was really nice and easy to talk to. At one point, we stopped walking and just stood still for several minutes, laughing and talking. He knew the Bible as much, if not more, than Foster. Brad seemed to get a kick out of being such a know-it-all.

He knew specifics about characters and stories in the Bible. My knowledge was limited to major Biblical figures, but nothing in real detail. What I did know at the time was learned in religion class or from TV.

I tried reading the King James version of the Bible before going to church with Brad and his family. The purpose was to impress him. It was difficult for me to understand because we didn't read from the Bible at my church. The priest gave his sermon and we listened. Plus, the words were written in a way that I didn't speak, and I couldn't relate to it.

Nonetheless, I didn't care what Brad thought about my lack of knowledge at that moment. It didn't matter what we talked about. I would have shown interest even if it bored me to death.

Time went by so quickly. Before I knew it, we arrived home. Mama was sitting in the living room with the door open, waiting. It was obvious she didn't like what she saw. While Brad was still standing there, an immediate explanation had to be given.

"Mama," I said in a careful tone of voice, "the church was having a second service and Ms. Loar knew you didn't give me permission to stay. She asked Brad to make sure I got home safely."

Mama said, "thank you Brad."

He was quite the gentleman saying, "Yes, ma'am, it was no problem."

I quickly said goodbye to Brad but not before asking if he would teach me more about the Bible. That was going to be my way to spend more time with him.

Brad agreed then turned and walked away.

I pretended not to be excited, but after going into the house, he invaded all my thoughts. That day, the next day, and the next. As a matter of fact, whenever I wasn't occupied or busy, he was all I thought about.

Shortly after that day, Foster came by. He made the mistake of sharing that Brad asked about me a few times. My ears perked up and the questions began.

"What did he say?" "Do you think he likes me?" "Who was the girl at church?"

I bombarded Foster with so many questions he just exploded and stormed off. That wasn't my concern. The only thing on my mind was Brad.

After a while, Foster stopped coming around. He seemed mad all the time and sarcastic about me liking his brother. It seemed like an attempt to make me feel guilty or something, but I didn't feel any sense of guilt.

Before storming off, Foster did me the favor of mentioning where Brad's bedroom was located in their house. I have no idea why he offered the information, but it was perfect. Brad's window faced my backyard.

One morning, after getting dressed, I went out back.

"There must be a God," I said aloud to myself!

His window was wide open with white curtains hanging out. *Hmmm, what could be done to accidentally on purpose get his attention?* Quite naturally, I did what any hormone-raging teenager would do. Positioned myself where I could clearly be seen and started yelling for my brothers. *Lol!* Of course, they didn't come running because I wasn't really yelling loud enough for them to hear me.

It worked! Brad stuck his head out the window and teasingly stated, "What you doin' all that yellin' for?"

Before knowing what would come out my mouth, I quickly responded, "Trying to get yo' attention."

"Is that right?" Brad replied.

"Yep," I said. "So you comin' down or what?"

Brad wasted no time coming down his backstairs into the backyard. We were separated by the tall fence that divided our properties, but it didn't stop us from talking.

This time, it had nothing to do with the Bible. We talked about school, basketball, his family, my family, and so on. During our conversation, the opportunity arrived to ask about miss holier-than-thou at his church.

"Was that your girlfriend?" I asked.

"Sometimes," he responded.

I couldn't help but laugh. "What do you mean sometimes?"

Brad was surprised at my maturity and said, "Why? You wanna be my girlfriend?"

My heart dropped but I kept it cool. Suddenly having the urge for him to know my intellect, I focused on speaking proper English.

"Why would anyone be interested in being your girlfriend when you're confused about having one already?"

I could tell he was impressed with my sarcasm and quick comebacks. We talked for about twenty-five minutes before ending the conversation. There was fear of getting caught by Mama, my uncle, or one of my brothers.

From that day forward, we became really good friends and talked all the time. Mostly sneaking because Mama was not as comfortable with our friendship like with me and Foster. She likely saw something in me that caused her concern. Maybe it was the stargazed look in my eyes. You know the one that girls get when their nose is wide open.

Brad and I eventually became a couple. Everyone, except Mama, thought we were perfect together. Love was in the air. We started spending more and more time together. It seemed the closer we got the more jealous I became.

Eventually, due to insecurities, I found myself becoming jealous of *other girls*. This included one of my closest friends, Marissa. After introducing her and Brad, they hit it off right away. I was thrilled until he commented on her attractiveness. It caused jealousy in a relationship where there shouldn't have been.

One day, Marissa asked to borrow my English notebook so she could get the homework assignment from a previous class. Without thinking, I gave it to her, completely forgetting about the poem describing my feelings. This deeply hurt her and ruined a perfectly good friendship. We stayed friends, but our relationship suffered and was never the same. It wasn't Marissa I didn't trust, but Brad.

I made the mistake of making him my everything. He was a mental security blanket. There was an unconscious need to mend my brokenness through someone else. This would later prove to be extremely harmful. No earthly person can take away the aftermath of trauma.

My relationship with Brad was causing an emotional dependency. Mama didn't like what she was seeing and tried to intervene. It was to no avail because my dread of losing him was greater than my fear of her. It caused a big rift between me and Mama, resulting in *defiance* on my part.

I became more persistent about spending time with Brad. Usually at church or while visiting with my play sister, Delores. This was often difficult since I was not allowed inside anyone's home without Mama's permission. Also, at least one of my brothers was frequently somewhere nearby. Interestingly enough, they were never required to accompany me to religious services.

At some point, church became a much bigger part of my life. I was going more frequently with Ms. Loar and my neighbors. This didn't cause me to lower my guard. There was still a lot of suspicion about *church folk* but learning more about the Bible was becoming enjoyable. It was no longer solely because I wanted to be with Brad. Other emotions grabbed my attention. My spirit started feeling things that couldn't be explained.

Even Mama saw a change in me. I had become more outgoing and less angry. There was a strong desire to gain knowledge, leading to me asking Mama about being baptized outside the Catholic church. She was initially skeptical but ended up giving her approval. This didn't happen without a strict condition.

"I expect you to maintain full membership at our church while experiencing other Christian denominations," Mama insisted.

Of course I quickly agreed to her stipulations, and tried my best to separate the two experiences. Paying attention at my church was becoming more difficult. I was learning so many things that conflicted with what was being taught.

This resulted in me refusing to go to confessional. Mama became irritated and insisted my rejection was about Brad, but it wasn't. She decided it was time to speak with our priest, which made me nervous. I really loved Father Manny but grew to dislike the solemn atmosphere of Sunday service.

Father was always very even-tempered and never seemed to be rattled by much of anything. This was no different. After Mama explained the situation, he gently asked why I was refusing to go to confessional. Looking at Mama, I hunched my shoulders (I don't know).

Before my mother could say anything, Father stopped her. He looked at me while speaking to Mama, and said, "It's okay, I really don't want her to be afraid and I'm curious."

After a few minutes, I said, "the Bible tells us we can speak directly with God, and he'll hear our prayers. We can have a conversation with Him to ask for forgiveness. That's why Christ died on the cross for us."

Father Manny leaned back in his chair and said, "Go on."

I explained how differently we prayed. The music made me feel like dancing and singing. It didn't feel that way at our church. People were always telling me to sit still, sing quietly and not say amen out loud. The only person that said it was okay for me to worship any way the spirit led was Ms. Simmons before she died.

She didn't like it when people told me to be quiet, so she'd sit next to me and sing even louder.

The next Sunday, after we met with Father Manny, he called me to the front of the church and told me to sing.

The look of confusion on my face spoke for itself. He whispered, "Sing your loud song."

Opening my mouth, I began singing my heart out. After it was over, Father praised me and told the whole church he wanted to hear that kind of praise every Sunday. He prohibited anyone from telling me to sing quietly again.

I couldn't wait to tell Brad about what happened at my church. He was excited and couldn't believe my priest had me singing gospel.

Some time after that, we formed a gospel choir. It was led by my high school choir director who was such a gifted musician.

My priest didn't stop there. At some point, the confessionals weren't used so much anymore. I have no clue if the changes happened because of our conversations or whether it was just time. Either way, I was glad.

Father would regularly meet with Mama and me to ask if I'd learned anything new. I was more than excited to share. We talked in detail about various stories in the Bible and my understanding of them.

It was clear to my mother that I was learning. She seemed happy. At the same time there seemed to be more uneasiness. As my knowledge got stronger, so did my need to be with Brad.

Admittedly, having a better understanding of the Bible made me that much closer to him, which Mama didn't like so much. Although she was pleased about my new-found passion for God, Mama did everything possible to keep me away from Brad. This included prohibiting me from going to church with Ms. Loar anymore.

The battle between us exploded into a full-blown war. I stopped sneaking around to see my boyfriend and boldly defied my mom's wishes. Things spiraled downward from there.

Technically, I was still a virgin, and she wanted to keep it that way. Mama tried all kinds of mean stuff to make Brad go away, like cutting off one of his braids.

He had long hair that was frequently worn French braided toward the back of his head. One day, we were sitting on my front porch with Mama. She suddenly got up and went into the house to get a pair of scissors. Mama warned him that he'd better leave, or she was going to cut his middle braid off, but Brad didn't move.

"You better get up because she's really going to cut your hair," I said.

Before anything else could come out my mouth, Mama cut his middle braid down to the back of his hairline. I couldn't believe she did that and neither could Brad. He didn't even get mad but just calmly got up and walked away.

I was furious but dared not say anything. That day, I mastered the art of giving the silent treatment, only speaking when spoken to with very short answers. Limited to yes or no if I could help it.

Brad may not have gotten mad but Ms. Loar sure was. More at him for sitting there letting it happen than at my mom. She figured Mama was just trying to protect me, like any good mother who plans for her child's future.

He ended up having to shave all his hair off because there was a big chunk missing. I thought for sure this would be the end of our relationship. Seems it only made us closer.

We survived that ordeal, but as time went on, Mama became more vocal about forbidding me to see Brad. She was convinced he was going to ruin my life by getting me pregnant.

I wasn't even thinking about having sex at the time. My past trauma made me fearful of that kind of intimacy and kept me from doing something stupid. Bill and Rocky took care of that. At least for a little while.

It was apparent I enjoyed my boyfriend's affection, but at the same time, it made me uncomfortable. I never told him about the abuse. Probably because there was still a lot of shame. I also believed he loved me so much that he would kill Bill and Rocky. Not telling him was the right decision, especially after he started making plans for us to get married.

Brad talked about going into the army and getting married after I completed high school, which was in about one year.

We were the perfect couple, and everyone except Mama thought marriage was a natural progression for our relationship. This included his mother and brothers who were just an extension of him.

I loved them all but had a special spot in my heart for his youngest brother, Dominique. Everyone called him Dom; however, I frequently referred to him as Baby Brother.

Dom and Brad were very close and somewhat attached at the hip. Baby Brother knew just about everything there was to know about his big bro. He was often the messenger and mediator between us as we begin experiencing some challenges in our love affair.

During a conversation with Baby Brother, he started talking about his nephew. We were laughing and joking for quite a while before he mentioned his nephew was Brad's son.

"What did you say?" I asked. "Did you say Brad has a son?"

All this time and not once did he mention anything about having a son. I refused to believe it. I turned to baby brother and said, "Stop lying. He would've told me something like that."

"Oh wow! You didn't know?" Baby Brother asked.

"No, I had no idea," was my response.

Dom honestly thought I already knew and looked fearful when it was clear I didn't.

That goes to show my naivety. Mama's fear came flooding to the forefront of my mind, except it wasn't me who got pregnant. Did she somehow know Brad already had a child?

I couldn't wait to confront him with the information. baby brother was asked to have him meet me in the backyard without giving a reason. There was nothing but tears and complete shock.

He came running down the back stairs of his house into the backyard with a smile on his face. His expression quickly changed as he saw the look on mine.

Before he could ask any questions, I lit into him. "You're a liar and a cheat," I began yelling. "Why didn't you tell me you had a son? Is it true?"

Brad was completely taken off guard as he confirmed it was true. My heart was broken, and all I could say was, "This whole time, not once did you mention a child."

"That's it! Men can't be trusted," I screamed. "You were supposed to be different (sobbing), but you're not. I never want to see or speak to you again."

I stormed off feeling like my heart had been ripped out of my chest. I was certain our relationship would never survive this.

As the weeks went on, it was hard not to think about Brad. I couldn't sleep and couldn't eat. Evidently, he was feeling the same way. Brad convinced Baby Brother to plead on his behalf. My initial reaction was to reject his offer. That thought quickly faded because living without him wasn't an option.

After we talked, he provided a genuine apology that convinced me he had not cheated. "It happened before we began *officially* dating," he cried.

What I said next amazed me. "So you just knocked some girl up? That's what condoms are made for!"

Brad looked like he was about to lose his best friend! If not for me being so young and inexperienced, he would have. For the little I knew about love, this was my first. Letting go wasn't so easy. Although the news was shocking, we moved past it.

I grew to respect Brad's love for his son. He was a good father. At least based on my limited knowledge regarding the traits of a good dad. This was a plus because I wanted children someday. Brad took pride in making sure his son had whatever he needed. That's why what happened a short time later was such a tragedy.

He received a call from his son's mother. There was some type of accident and he needed to get to the hospital right away. At the time, his son was a small toddler.

Somehow the little guy was able to access the family's swimming pool and accidently fell in. By the time the family located him, it was too late. This was a very painful time for Brad. I was so glad we rectified our differences. Not being there for him during that time would have been unbearable. He was my everything!

Splintered Pieces

The splintered pieces of defeat are trampled about like leaves on the ground. They blow here and there as strong winds whisk them to their next destination. Where will they end up? Who will gather the pieces to make them whole again? How beautiful they could be if someone took time to restore their Mosaic form. The colors of falls beauty gone too quickly as the seasons change.

Chapter 7

Friendship and Sunset

After the tragic situation with Brad's son, I had a sudden desire to make changes to my appearance. Life was too short.

I began experiencing a transformation and wanted my sweetheart to see me differently. My wardrobe became form fitting and the urge to have a more attractive appearance was priority. Although makeup was not really my thing at the time, I wanted to learn how to apply it like the other girls.

What a blessing to have a childhood friend like Liz. We had been besties since kindergarten. She was one of the people in my life that I completely trusted.

My friend had this flawless way of applying makeup. I was really embarrassed about asking her to show me how to do it.

Liz chuckled and said, "Girl, I had to learn, and that's why I'm your best friend."

Thinking back, she arched my eyebrows with a straight razor (guess me and blades were meant to be). That was some scary stuff. As far as I knew, straight razors were for cutting people when necessary.

"Here goes!" she said.

After both eyebrows were arched, Liz put alcohol on some cotton balls to prevent infection and explained how it might sting a little. She was supposed to give me a warning before cleansing the area. Well, there was no warning.

Her hand was so quick I didn't even see it coming. While screaming from the burning sensation on my right eyebrow, she hit me with the left swipe. It was hilarious. I laughed so hard my stomach hurt. The girl was Quick Draw McGraw.

After the burning sensation went away, Liz applied my makeup and wouldn't let me see until her masterpiece was complete. She stood there for a few minutes in awe. I didn't know what that look was all about and panicked.

"What's wrong?," I said.

She said, "Nothing's wrong, you're just really pretty."

Now I thought Liz was trying to be funny. The one thing I wasn't…was pretty.

Like a professional she pulled out a mirror and said, "Close your eyes." When the mirror was directly in front of my face, she said, "Now open."

I just sat there, amazed, and kept looking at Liz then back at the mirror. Wow! For the first time, my smile was surrounded by something more attractive.

That one act of kindness by my dear friend meant more to me than a pot of gold. She was proud of her artistic makeover. However, I can't say she was thrilled about the reason I was making such a change.

Brad would love my new look. I wanted to surprise him because he was preparing to go into the military. This was my opportunity to present myself as his lovely future bride.

After Liz helped me see my outward beauty, I started saving my allowance and buying new clothes and makeup. Trying a little bit of this and a little bit of that until I had the perfect look. This would surely cause Brad's heart to almost pound out of his chest.

Indeed, he was noticeably impressed after witnessing my transformation. His eyes were glazed with delight as he proudly scooped me into his arms and declared his undying love. My makeup was flawless and the outfit I selected slightly showed some of the curves I had been hiding.

Brad took a step back and said, "Girl, you *gon'* hurt somebody looking like that. I don't want to leave you here by yourself."

While blushing, I quickly responded, "Just remember what you *comin'* home to."

"It would be impossible to forget my baby," Brad said in a teasing tone of voice before hugging me again.

Feeling attractive, I desired nothing more than being with my future husband. My heart wanted to trust him but feared he would find someone else. Who would I be without him? He was my all!

Before long, the day came when Brad had to ship out for boot camp. It was harder than I thought to say goodbye. I cried uncontrollably and felt a deep pain in the pit of my stomach.

I called Liz to tell her how pleased Brad was with my makeover. It didn't take long before I started bawling because he was gone. Liz just talked in a calm and soothing voice until I stopped crying.

It's so funny how opposites really do attract. She was the peaceful half of our friendship and I was the storm. We were always there for each other, no matter what. This would prove to be a lifetime sisterhood.

Friendship and Sunset

The love of a true friend is like the beauty of
witnessing the sunset in the evening sky. No words
can describe its awesomeness. If only time could
stand still so we never have to see it disappear into the night.

The power of love between friends is like the power of an
extraordinary sunset. You can't feel or see it all the time, but you
know it's there. Though its distance is galaxies away, it remains
within arm's reach. Waiting to return and bring joy to those who
encounter it. Always illuminating rays of warmth and comfort.

We miss the sunset
when it's not around only to be overjoyed with awe when it
returns. Never wanting to lose sight of how it was shaped and
formed into something special. That's Friendship and Sunset!

Chapter 8

A Mother's Love

Admittedly, even though there was an outward change, I still maintained the feeling of ugliness inside. There was an ongoing battle with poor self-esteem and lack of self-worth, but I was determined to win the fight.

Brad and Liz weren't the only ones who witnessed my change. Mama also saw that I was growing up, and it must have scared her. She became more protective and watchful. I couldn't breathe. It didn't even matter that Brad was gone. Why didn't she trust me?

It seemed Mama was always fussing about something. Anything! It baffled me as to why, but I was becoming fed up with being treated like a baby.

Finally, a situation arose that I decided it was time to *buck* (fight) back.

Mama had to run an errand and instructed me and my brothers to stay in the house until she returned. Me and Dray stayed in the house until Ms. Loar called and asked if I could babysit little Johnny (her godson) for a short time. Watching Johnny was nothing new, so I figured it would be no big deal and went next door to get him. Boy, that proved to be the wrong decision!

When my mother returned home she initially seemed okay with seeing Johnny playing in the living room floor. After about twenty-five minutes, it hit her.

She abruptly stormed out of her bedroom and asked, "how did Johnny get here?"

My voice was low and cautious. "I went next door to get him. You said it was okay for me to babysit whenever Ms. Loar needed someone to keep Johnny."

Mama became furious and demanded he be taken home.

It just wasn't right. Turning to my mother I said "What did I do wrong? But you said"—(slap).

She never gave me a chance to challenge what I felt was wrong on her part. By this time anger set in and a fighting spirit took over. I took Johnny home and decided it was time to stand up to Mama.

After returning, Mama demanded I go to my room.

"What? I'm too old for punishments," I responded.

I stood there with my fist balled then thought better of it but refused to go to my room. My defiance sent her into a rage.

This was my first time seeing Mama so mad. It baffled me because my oldest brother still hadn't returned home yet, and she never asked where he was. Then again, he was a young adult now.

She was like a mad woman who'd lost her mind for no apparent reason. Mama stormed out of the room and returned with a broom.

Was she really going to hit me with that broom? I snapped! It was out of sheer fear and reflex that I grabbed the broom, knocked Mama to the floor, and raised the hard end to strike her.

Just then Dray came running in the room, yelling. "Bree, what are you doing? Put the broom down."

I couldn't really understand what he was saying because my anger was so out of control. It seemed like things were happening in slow motion. The only thing that came to mind was I've tried to do everything asked of me. I didn't drop out of school. I didn't get pregnant, and I had the best reputation of all the girls in my neighborhood but that wasn't enough.

I was so angry and wanted to tell her that the only men who ever violated me was the one she let into our home and the other sick person in our neighborhood. My flesh wanted to hurt her like she was trying to hurt me. The rage inside was like an out-of-control fire.

I don't know what made me look directly into Mama's face. Maybe it was something Dray was yelling because she was definitely afraid.

That's when reality kicked in. I was standing over Mama with the handle raised high above my head, ready to come down with all my might. Shame caused me to drop the broom and run out the house.

I don't remember much after that except Dray was afraid to leave for college from fear of us hurting each other.

Something broke in me that day. The thought of standing over my mother about to strike her made me sick to my stomach. I had never outright stood up to Mama before. It was quite an experience for both of us.

Thankfully, we got past that day. Dray eventually went to college, and my mother never raised her hand to me again. She started talking to, instead of at me. It was becoming easier for us to communicate.

It was obvious she wanted to apologize but didn't know quite what to say. My mom even started asking about Brad. I didn't know what to think and decided to go with it.

She became like another best friend as we started having deep conversations about any and everything. Mama was so proud of me preparing to graduate high school and cautiously urged me to take some time to finish college before getting married. I agreed to talk with Brad about waiting when he returned home.

A Mother's Love

Who can understand it? Who can judge it?
I long to hear the sound of sweetness from her voice.
The voice of love that draws me to her presence. I
embrace the passion of her protective nature. A mother's
love is unfailing. It moves in ways that the mind
cannot comprehend. Flowing from the depths

of the ocean and reaching as high as the sky. Her prayers travel over mountains and through valleys to provide a covering. Who can fathom her perseverance? Who can challenge her love? Who can despise a mother's love?

Chapter 9

Shattered

My senior year in high school was quickly coming to an end. Brad had been in the army for about a year. We kept in touch by writing and was excited about really having a chance to spend some quality time together.

Based on his last letter, he would be coming home for a few weeks. Our time together was sure to be special. I didn't know what to expect but was positive it would be memorable.

Brad was the only person I ever wanted to be with. It never crossed my mind that someone else might be attracted to me. I just always wondered what Brad saw.

Imagine my surprise when one of my classmates, Karlos, and I started flirting with each other. I didn't even realize we were flirting. All my thoughts were always about getting married and living happily ever after with Brad. Karlos was not a part of that plan.

It started very innocently in a trio friendship. Karlos, Julian, and I were basketball buddies. We could often be found in the gym during lunch hour and other free periods.

We were all very studios and never got in trouble at school. At least until Karlos and I were caught joking around in class. Our desks were side by side. Karlos reached over to hit me. Just as I reached to hit him back, the teacher turned and caught me. We did what any teenage boy and girl would do. Blamed each other. It didn't work because we both were given Saturday detention. That was a consequence given to students required to go to school on Saturday.

We thought our parents would be really upset because his father was just as strict as Mama, but we survived. Julian teased me for a long time. He had never gotten detention and was proud of it.

They both treated me like a buddy, so I was puzzled when things started feeling a little different. Our interaction started changing when we began exercising together.

Karlos and I were both kind of chunky and decided to start working on our weight. The baby fat began melting off, and his muscles became evident. I'd already started becoming more comfortable with my shape. Losing weight provided the confidence needed for improved self-esteem. Apparently, Karlos took notice too.

There was a serious attraction brewing, although neither of us admitted it at the time. He was somewhat shy and my heart was still with Brad.

My thoughts needed to stay focused on our time together when he came home. It was kind of hard to do while in class with Karlos every day. I remember thinking, *I just have to make it through final exams then everything will be okay. God, please help me be strong so I don't do anything stupid.* It was much easier said than done as the attraction continued to get stronger.

This was too much stress for me to be so young. My mind was suddenly confused about something I'd always been so sure about— my relationship with Brad.

Thankfully, commencement day arrived just in time. I felt like a queen. My dress was nicely fitted, and my makeup was perfect (Thank you, Liz).

There was a readiness to put this day behind me so Brad and I could move on with our lives. The big eighteen was in about five months and all the answers were clear. In my mind, I was ready for marriage, even though mama asked me to speak with Brad about waiting.

Graduation day intensified an already powerful attraction. Karlos was taking his weight lifting very seriously. Even his nicely fitted suit couldn't hide all the muscles. As the ceremony went on, there were so many sparks flying between us, it could have started a forest fire.

I would glance over at Karlos, then he'd glance over at me. We'd both blush and smile like two little kids. Not much was heard from the speakers on that day. I was either daydreaming about Brad or being flirtatious with Karlos.

When the day ended, it was hard deciding whether to be relieved or disappointed. There was more confusion now than ever before. *How would I feel once Brad arrived home?*

It didn't take long for me to find out. While sitting on the front porch talking to some friends, I saw a man walking in our direction. There was no doubt in my mind it was Brad with his bowlegs, cool stride, and army fatigues. As he got closer, I screamed his name and ran straight into his arms. It seemed like we held on to each other for dear life.

Brad was so handsome, distinguished, and looked like he'd been working out. He was always muscular, but something about his uniform made his physique stand out even more.

Mama came outside to see what all the commotion was about. I froze momentarily, not knowing what her reaction would be.

She looked at Brad and said, "Welcome home, soldier."

Whew! A sigh of relief!

After spending just moments together, it was confirmed that he was the one I wanted to be with. Brad was the person I was willing to share my world with. To share my heart and even my body.

The goal was to wait until after we got married before having sex, but I gave in to the fear of losing Brad. It led to me losing my virginity to someone who became my everything. It was a decision that would turn into years of regret.

If only I knew then what would later be revealed. If only I were stronger in my spiritual walk. If only I had listened to Mama. If only...

When it got closer to the time for Brad to leave, it felt like something was about to change between us. I didn't quite know what it was, but decided to make the best of our time while he was home.

When the day arrived for Brad to return for duty, we said our goodbyes. In the blink of an eye, he was gone.

After about a week, I was missing him so much it felt difficult to breathe. Baby brother tried helping but nothing worked. Probably because we both missed the person our hearts loved so deeply.

I started spending more time with his mom because it made me feel closer to him. We talked about all the challenges Brad and I overcame, but she said something that floored me. I'm sure, just like Baby Brother in another situation, she assumed he told me.

Ms. Loar was laughing about when Brad told her he'd gotten somebody pregnant. She was terrified thinking it was me. Her fear was Mama would kill him. Ironically, this seemed to be a common theme when it came to my mom and uncle.

I laughed and said "Nope, it wasn't me. We were careful."

Ms. Loar just shook her head as she stated, "At least he was careful with you." She took a deep breath before continuing. "He should have learned his lesson the first time around."

I froze as if time had suddenly stopped. *"Huh? What are you talking about?"* I responded.

She saw the look on my face and realized her mistake as she asked, "What did you think I was talking about?"

"His son that drowned in the pool, right?" I replied.

Brad's mom immediately became angry after realizing he never told me. She just kept saying, "I told him he'd better tell you. He should have told you he fathered a set of twin boys."

Shaking and somewhat hysterical, the only thing that came out my mouth was "Mama was right! How could he do this to me, *again*? All that talk about getting married was a lie."

Ms. Loar tried to tell me how much her son loved me. My heart wasn't feeling that! She insisted Brad did something stupid but he loved me.

Love? If that's love, I can live without it. Who needs that kind of disappointment!

Devastated, angry and wanting to hurt someone, my mind was flooded with ways to get back at Brad. *That's it! Let's see how he likes having his heart ripped out and broken.* I was sick of everybody throwing the word *love* around like it was a baseball.

Quite naturally, I called Liz to tell her about all the drama. She was really mad that Brad hurt me so deeply and said, "It's his loss. He didn't deserve you anyway."

My friend was spot-on! Although there was a lot of pain, I agreed and replied, "You're right, I'm way too good for him. What was going on in my head?" We both laughed. My next words were, "I know one thing, if a man doesn't treat me like my brothers, uncle and grandfather then he better keep it *movin!*"

"That's right," Liz responded.

After our conversation ended, I thought about how the men in my family had unwavering love for me, especially my grandfather. As a small child, I asked Grandpa if he was going to marry me. He laughed and tried his best to explain marriage in an age appropriate way. No matter what he said, my mind was made up that we would be married. Grandpa finally gave up and simply said "okay baby."

That's why, in the midst of the situation with Brad, the roof came crashing in when we learned Grandpa had suddenly become ill.

Mama received word that my grandfather was in the hospital and not doing so well. I went into a depressive state. First finding out that the person I loved didn't really love me back. Now the person who truly loved me was at risk of dying.

The doctors didn't think he would make it. Mama immediately packed our suitcases, and we headed down south to Birmingham, Alabama. On the plane, I kept thinking about all the good times we had over the summers and school breaks, spending time with the patriarch of our family. He was so proud about letting everyone know we were his grandchildren and addressed Mama as his daughter, not daughter-in-law.

Grandpa also made no secret about letting my brothers know that I was his baby girl. He would say, "boys have to grow up to be men, but girls are supposed to be taken care of."

While that was old school thinking, I liked the fact that my brothers were taught to look out for me.

It's one of the reasons there was such an emotional attachment to Brad. He was a protector and provider like my grandfather. Now I felt nothing but disrespect for him. At the same time my heart was breaking from fear of losing another loved one.

We arrived in Birmingham and made our way to the hospital. Grandpa looked very weak. This scared me because he was a very tall and strong-looking man even in his older age.

What happened next is a bit fuzzy, but Mama was hurting in a way we weren't used to seeing her. Heartbroken! Grandpa was the only father she had ever really known who truly loved her as a daughter. My mom was sexually abused by her stepfather, causing her to leave home at an early age. That explains why she was so overprotective of me.

We stayed in Alabama for about a week with the intent on coming back to stay a little longer. That never happened. Shortly after returning home, Mama received a call that Grandpa made his transition.

I was crushed, and by this time, the storm inside me had returned with a vengeance. It was furiously raging out of control with nowhere constructive for it to be released. Grandpa was dead, Brad betrayed me and my heart was shattered into small little pieces.

Shattered

Pieces of hurt and pain scattered here and there like leaves blowing in the wind.
I don't know if I can break free from the chains of this rage I'm feeling again.
There is no net to catch the droplets of fury raging inside of me.
There are no words of comfort that can stop what's bound to be.
Fragments of my mind have been shattered like bits of broken glass.
I'm sinking, I'm drowning, how long will this pain last?
I'm like a wounded animal, bruised, beaten and battered.
Virtue lost, life gone, mind weakened…Shattered!

Chapter 10

Fix My Brokenness

A short time following the ordeal with Brad and my grandfather's death, I became focused on going to college. My future would be moving forward without Brad, only he didn't know it yet. He had to do a year before returning home again. I'd deal with him then. I was in no mood to hear any more lies. I was done trying to be *good*.

Being *a good girl* wasn't working for me. It didn't work when Bill wormed his way into our home. It didn't work when Rocky tried to cause harm. It didn't work when Brad broke my heart. *Later for that…* It was time to make my own choices.

I gave into my physical attraction for Karlos and threw caution to the wind. The more time we spent together, the less time I thought about anything or anyone else. I didn't even consider what Mama would think if she caught us, which she eventually did.

Mama set a trap. It would've worked if the upstairs door hadn't gotten stuck. She suspected I was sneaking someone in the house, but had no idea Brad and I were no longer a couple.

One day Good old mom announced she was going shopping and would be returning in a few hours. This seemed strange because it was getting dark. Dray was now at college and Tony was in the military. Although I was just about Eighteen, Mama still had the habit of having my uncle keep an eye out in her absence.

There was a critical piece of information she left out. One of our neighbors was to watch for any unusual activity and notify her if they saw anything. Karlos and I stepped right into her trap. My neighbor saw him arrive and head towards the backyard. He parked his bike before coming in through the back of the house.

About forty-five minutes later, we heard someone coming through the front door. Karlos quickly hid in the closet and I pretended to be asleep. Mama walked into my bedroom, which was now near the backdoor, off the kitchen. I had moved into Tony's old room after he went into the armed services.

"Hi, just wanted to let you know I was home," Mama said as she looked around the room.

My only response was, "Okay."

After saying goodnight my mother cut off all the lights in the house except the Kitchen. This was weird, but it didn't hit me at the time. She headed back to her room, which was by the front door, and turned off the lights there too.

After a few minutes, I checked to make sure the coast was clear. After opening the closet door, Karlos wasted no time getting to the back exit. Just as he was sneaking out, Uncle Bob was trying to open the upstairs door. It was stuck.

We were so naïve and didn't even realize the light in the kitchen was designed to be a spotlight. Mama saw the whole thing from her bedroom and notified my uncle who was waiting upstairs.

Karlos moved so fast that by the time my uncle got the door open, he was on his bike and halfway down the back alley. That was the kind of risks we were willing to take. It felt like love at the time. It always does when we give so much of ourselves to someone.

Mama didn't say anything about what she witnessed that night until about a month later. We were having a deep discussion about relationships when Mama asked what happened with Brad.

"What do you mean what happened," I asked?

She just smiled before saying, "You were ready to get married a short while ago, and now you're dating someone else."

With obvious shock on my face I responded, "How did you know?"

"You're not as slick as you think you are," Mama stated. "Go ahead and tell me what happened."

After giving the details of how Brad broke my heart, she was genuinely sad for me. Mama then disclosed her suspicions about my relationship with Brad being over. It's also when she admitted knowing I was having company in the house and her plans to catch us in the act. It was completely baffling as to why she let me believe we had gotten away with it.

My mother cautioned me to enjoy being young and not get into another serious relationship too soon. Common sense told me she was right, but I was still in search of finding happiness through someone else.

Once again wise words fell on death ears. Karlos and I continued to grow closer and talked frequently. It was rare that a day went by and we did not communicate. This continued when I enrolled in a local private college and lived on Campus.

Karlos was constantly on my mind and I missed him so much. My initial reaction was to go back home with Mama. At least we would be able to see each other more frequently.

This mindset slightly changed as I started meeting new people. Going home was contemplated less frequently as I settled into a routine. It wasn't long before I started enjoying my new-found freedom. I'd never been away from home before and it felt good.

Mama was nervous about me being on my own, even though I was attending a local college. Her mind was eased after meeting my dorm director, Shelly. She was like a big sister and kept an eye out for a group of us. We were so rowdy and rambunctious.

The school year was in session a little over a month. My relationship with Karlos was strong, and my mom was still getting use to being an empty nester.

Everything was perfect until my brother Tony showed up at my dorm. He had gotten out of the military, was married and expecting a child. Tony also had a heavy drinking problem. Enlisting was supposed to help him become more responsible and gain control. Seems it had the exact opposite effect.

My brother looked really disheveled, and his appearance was embarrassing. I pleaded with him to leave before my friends showed up.

Tony kept saying "I love you sis. Can't I just visit with my lil sis."

"No," I said in a harsh tone. "You've been drinking, and you stink."

He eventually stumbled away, walking toward the bus stop drunk. I was relieved and thought nothing more of it. Likely because of being preoccupied with thinking about Karlos and the celebration Shelly helped put together.

My eighteenth birthday would be in two weeks, and a toga party had been planned for that weekend. I was so excited because I'd never been to a toga party before.

As it got later in the evening, exhaustion got to me. I laid down and let my mind race with all the thoughts of how much fun the party would be.

Before long, I drifted off to sleep but was awakened by horrifying screams. My suitemate ran into the room, yelling, "What's wrong? What's wrong?"

At first, I was a little dazed and not fully awake. Unexpectedly the residents from across the hall came running into the room, and somebody ran to get Shelly. She rushed into the room to see what all the commotion was about.

The screams were mine. I was freaking out trying to tell them about my nightmare.

There was an awful car crash, and somebody was in the passenger seat. Their face was blurred, but it had to be someone close to me. I needed to figure out who it was to warn them.

Shelly helped me calm down and wouldn't leave until I agreed it was just a dream. In my heart, I knew better. It was always more than just a dream! The images were too vivid.

My first thought was to call Karlos, but I didn't think he'd understand. We had never talked about anything like this before and he would probably think I was weird.

After a couple days, I forced myself to push it out of my memory and thought about the upcoming toga party.

There was a lot of hustle and bustle to get ready for the big day. All of the planning was well worth the wait.

It was the bomb! Everyone had sheets tied around their shoulders, and carrying torches. We laughed, ate, and acted silly all night.

At some point, I decided to turn in for the night. Just as I reached for the remote to turn on the TV, several people burst into my room. They strongly encouraged me to go back to the party. It was my birthday, and they wanted to make sure every second was enjoyed, so we all returned to the party.

It must have lasted until 2 a.m., which was nothing unusual for some folks. When it was over, I had no problem sleeping off all the excitement.

The phone rang early the next morning. It was Shelly calling to instruct me to pack all my things because my uncle would be picking me up.

Huh? What? I was confused and didn't understand why she was telling me to get packed.

I kept asking, "What's wrong? What's wrong?"

Shelly wouldn't answer over the phone, but finally came to my room, realizing an explanation had to be given. She reassured me everything was fine before stating, "Your mom is sick and was taken to the hospital."

Nothing else needed to be said. My bags were packed as fast as humanly possible. I immediately called Karlos to let him know about the situation and waited for my uncle.

When he arrived, I was full of questions. "Where's Mama?" "How is she doing?" "What happened?"

Uncle Bob just kept saying "She's doing fine, don't worry."

There was something wrong, but I couldn't put my finger on it.

Instead of going to check on my mom, we went to my childhood home where Uncle Bob, my cousins, and aunt were living on the first level. By this time my niece, Scha'Kerra (Ke-Ke) had been born. Tony and his wife (Shirley) lived in the second level with their infant daughter.

We pulled up to the house, and Shirley was sitting in the front window upstairs. She looked very sad.

I jokingly said to her, "Where's my brother? Tell him he owes me a birthday card."

She immediately perked up and said, "Okay."

I asked again, "Where is he?"

Her response was simply, "I don't know."

Me and my uncle went into the house where my aunt and cousins were sitting. They looked like somebody had just died. I was getting frustrated.

"*Why is everyone acting so depressed?*" I said. "*No one wished me a happy birthday. Is my mother okay?*"

Suddenly everyone perked up. By this time, my mind had become more suspicious. There was something they weren't telling me. I demanded my uncle take me home to see Mama.

After a short period of time, we got back in the car and drove toward the city airport. When he pulled into the driveway, I didn't even wait until the car stopped before jumping out and running into the house. Mama was standing at the sink with her back turned toward the door.

Completely puzzled, I asked, "When did you get out of the hospital?"

Mama's back was facing me when she softly said, "That's just what they said to get you home."

Panic started overcoming me. I looked around and saw different members of my family blocking all the exits.

Mama abruptly swung around and said, "He's dead. Your brother's dead."

I didn't know which brother she was referencing. My first thought was Dray because he was away at college. It didn't matter, I started screaming and running. There was a need to get out of there, but all the doors were blocked.

My mind was racing. Before long, I took a run toward the nearest window prior to being tackled to the ground. It was my only out, and I was ready to go right through it to break free. My dream was true. It all came flooding back. I became that much more upset.

The only words that came out were, "I told them somebody was going to die. I told them, Mama, I told them. Nobody would believe me."

My mother kept saying, "I know, baby. I know."

My family held me down for what seemed like hours until they got me calm. After a while, I was finally able to ask, "Which brother?"

Mama softly said, "Tony."

My heart started shattering. He just wanted to see me. I made him go away and never said I love you.

"They shouldn't have been able to convince me it was just a dream," I cried. It was clear that someone I knew was in the passenger seat of a blue car that crashed into a brick building. "Is that how he died?"

Everyone except my mother and uncle were shocked. My aunt asked, "How'd you know?"

I buried my face in Mama's chest and cried uncontrollably. She knew that ever since childhood, my dreams and visions frequently came true.

The last memory of my oldest brother was how horribly I treated him out of embarrassment. There was a lot of guilt for celebrating my birthday at the same time my brother was dying.

It was a little later when I learned that my uncle called Shelly the night of the toga party. He asked her to keep me occupied and away from the television. The accident was all over the news.

Shelly told my uncle about the dream. She cried while explaining how I tried to tell everyone someone close to me was going to die.

He simply responded "She's always been sensitive like that. Feeling and knowing things that couldn't be explained."

My dorm director was amazed! If she had not witnessed it for herself, the whole situation would have been unbelievable. There was no doubt in her mind that my dream would make Tony's homegoing that much more difficult for me, and it was.

Planning Tony's funeral was distressing and took a toll on all of us. I shut down and would barely communicate with anyone except Karlos and Liz. Dray was devastated and a part of Mama died in that car crash with Tony. I could hear her crying at night asking God, *"why?"*

Mama was experiencing a deep-rooted pain that no parent should ever have to go through. Preparing to say her final good-bye was no easy task. Somehow, she managed to press forward. What a strong woman!

As we were writing Tony's obituary, Mama did something that took all of us by surprise. When listing his siblings, she included Diane. Turns out there was a good reason my dad insisted we meet our sister. She and Tony were hanging in the same crowd and becoming pretty good friends. Daddy didn't want them to end up dating each other. My brother was a popular guy, so I could see how that would've become problematic.

On the day of his funeral, there was standing room only. His fraternity brothers were lined all around the walls of the church. We didn't even know he pledged. There were a lot of people I hadn't seen for years and others who were unknown altogether.

Following service, the procession line was so long I couldn't see where it ended. I knew my brother was well-liked, but had no clue just how many people loved and respected him.

When everything was over, I spent a few weeks with Mama before going back to school. After returning, it was difficult to concentrate and remain engaged. I just couldn't forgive myself for not being more attentive to my dream.

Staying in school was difficult and my grades suffered tremendously. I couldn't focus which caused a lot of frustration. The dean of student affairs heard about my family's tragedy and refused to impose an academic dismissal. She allowed an additional semester to improve. It was to no avail. I left the college when the term ended. Dropping out was the only alternative.

My mom wanted me to move back home, but that wasn't a realistic choice. I'd gotten used to my freedom, and my relationship with Mama was better than ever, so we compromised.

Shirley moved back to Guam with my niece shortly after the funeral. The upstairs flat in my childhood home was now vacant.

Mama agreed I could move in and understood it would help me feel
closer to my brother. We both needed our own space to grieve.

Fix My Brokenness

I look for love, trying to see the beauty in
me through someone else's eyes.
I feel like nobody, desiring to be somebody,
wearing a smile of disguise.
I keep hearing you call my name like a quiet whisper in the night.
Let me in! I want to be the reason you anxiously await the daylight.
But anger and hatred have become my drug
of choice, down to my very core.
My mind battles love and hate like that old game of tug of war.
There's that familiar rage fueling my existence,
knocking loudly at the door.

The sound of shattering is my heart breaking
like tiny little pieces of glass.
I'm falling, I'm fading, somebody please help me,
my future is moving back into my past.
The barriers are trying to surround me, and
they're as fierce as Jericho's walls.
Where is courage? Where is power? Where is
victory? I'm desperately seeking them all.

Darkness tries to overtake me under this cumulonimbus cloud.
But some rain has got to fall because the
rushing of a mighty wind is loud.
Oh God! I need your refreshing water, but
your name I'm too ashamed to speak.
The pieces of my mind are like a puzzle that I
can't find, my spirit is worn and weak.
I need you to fix my brokenness so that
I will no longer be shattered.

Gather little fragments of my brokenness so
they will no longer be scattered.
I want to become stronger and be the person I was designed to be.
With mended cracks, healed wounds, and
my purpose chasing after me.

Chapter 11

Choices

When trauma and tragedy occur, we can become stuck in varying stages of grief. Mine was anger. A vicious cycle of self-destructive behavior and rage slowly picking up momentum one situation after another.

Following Tony's death, I looked for ways to overcome the feeling of darkness inside me. It felt like my entire being was falling into a black hole that was as deep as a bottomless pit. Who would be able to understand the tornado that was brewing? There had to be a way to overcome this feeling of hopelessness.

I chose to handle my sorrow by spending more time with Liz and other people that really cared about me. This included Karlos and Julian.

Karlos and I started spending more time with each other again and enrolled in a local community college together. As our attraction became more noticeable to Julian, he (Julian) started changing, always making sarcastic remarks. An obvious sign of jealousy. In a way, it was cute. He was feeling a little left out, so I made it a point to spend time with him whenever possible.

It was easy since we lived so close to each other. I'd hang with him at the neighborhood recreation center or just sit around talking with his family. It wasn't unusual for me to steer clear of any conversation about Karlos to minimize hurt feelings.

Sometime in midsummer things came to a head. Everything happened so fast. The need to be with Karlos was like an addiction. When I was with him, it made me forget about Brad, Grandpa, Tony and all the pain inside me. Spending weekends together and talking on the phone was the norm.

I had no intention of opening my heart to anyone again, especially not so soon but it just happened. At the time, I didn't really understand the blurred line of love and lust. It felt like my heart was mending.

The anger inside me seemed to be fading away, but it wasn't. I was just substituting one emotion for another. Wearing a more profound mask of smiles. Once again becoming dependent on someone else to validate me.

Karlos always kept me laughing so I associated that feeling with happiness. Being with him provided a sense of normalcy. Regrettably, once again putting all my confidence in another human being to rid myself of unshakable pain. It worked for a while and all was well.

Everything was going perfectly and moving in the right direction until Brad came home. This time, *joy* was not the word that came to mind.

Brad had still been writing letters and didn't appear to know about Tony or what his mom revealed. There was some unfinished business that needed to be settled.

Karlos was aware of Brad but never seemed concerned. Likely because he was hundreds of miles away. I got the sense that Brad coming home made Karlos feel a little more uncomfortable, but he knew this day would eventually arrive.

I didn't know what would be said. However, there was no doubt our relationship had come to an end. The trust bond was broken, and there was no opportunity for another strike. It was time for me to pitch a curve ball of my own.

My soon to be ex-boyfriend came over to my place. I greeted him with a smile and half-hearted hug. We sat on the sofa as he began telling me all about his adventures. Brad got to the part of the conversation about us getting married. After the wedding, he would make plans for me to move wherever he was stationed.

This was the part of the discussion I could no longer allow to go on. There was something he needed to know.

We talked about how much love and respect I always had for him, but my feelings were different now.

He needed to feel what it was like to hurt so deeply that you could hardly breathe. I never mentioned my knowledge of his sons, only that I no longer wanted to be with him.

Brad was hurt and tears welled up in his eyes. That's when he revealed to me that one of our neighbors wrote him about me seeing someone else.

My blood was boiling. *"How dare she! What gave her the right?"* I yelled.

While someone was keeping an eye on me, no one kept an eye on him. She was going to get a piece of my mind, but that would have to wait until later.

He didn't appear to be angry, just hurt. It was at that very moment I regretted my actions. Unfortunately, pride would not allow me to apologize. In my immature mind, I believed he should be begging for my forgiveness instead of acting all hurt.

Brad asked, "Is there anything I can do to make our relationship work? I really love you."

Wanting to scream I thought, *if you loved me, why did you get somebody else pregnant again!*

I refused to lose my composure. Instead, my mouth spoke words that shocked even me—to insult him as a man. I will never repeat it, just trust. It was wrong but it was done!

That day, our relationship officially came to an end. Brad returned to the military, and I felt completely free to continue pursuing my relationship with Karlos.

It felt like we were closer than ever, as if that were possible. We talked about everything under the sun. This included what would happen if by some fluke the unexpected occurred.

The conversation started with an intense question "What would we do if I ever got pregnant?"

"Well abortion is out of the question, because I don't believe in that," Karlos stated.

"Would you want to keep the baby?" I asked.

He quickly replied, "It would be my baby, of course."

"Well I don't think abortion is right either. I would probably just leave town without telling anybody."

Surprised, Karlos asked, "Why would you do that?"

"I don't know," was the only answer that came to mind.

We both laughed and continued building what appeared to be a great relationship and even better friendship. I was pretty sure Karlos loved me because I was his first.

One day, it dawned on me that Karlos had never said those magic words. Being a very upfront person, I asked him, "Do you love me?"

His response was "Yes."

The expectation was that he would say yes, I love you, but those words never came out of his mouth. I took a different approach and was more specific about the response that was desired.

Looking Karlos directly in his eyes I said, "Say it. Tell me you love me."

He refused to say the words. Red flags went up and insecurity kicked in. I was upset but for whatever reason, the relationship didn't end. Without really knowing it, I started secretly building walls and spending more time with other friends, like Julian.

He had feelings for me, and I took advantage of our friendship. Having my emotional needs met was all that mattered. It was insensitive of me not to consider how my actions might be impacting him.

We were close and he loved having me around but was basically given an ultimatum. Either accept and respect my relationship with Karlos or our friendship had to be terminated. He was clear that having me in his life as a friend was better than not having me at all. From that point forward, we were cool about everything, so I thought.

Although committed to Karlos, I started having insecurities about his love for me. It began causing resistance on my part. To the point of not wanting to spend as much time together anymore.

Remembering the last time we went to our special place is painful. It was spontaneous and I didn't want to go, but Karlos was so persistent. I shouldn't have given in.

"Come on, let's just go this last time," Karlos insisted.

Looking at Karlos I said, "Did you bring any protection with you?"

"No, but it's just this one time"

Unable to believe what was coming out of his mouth I replied, "It only takes one time to get pregnant."

Karlos, looked so dejected that I gave in, knowing it was a risk we shouldn't have taken.

That was the last time Karlos and I ever spent intimate time together. We continued to talk on the phone and hang out. However, it was getting to the point my body was tired a lot. I was sleeping all the time and not wanting to do much.

Oh no! I missed my cycle. *This can't be happening.* We always used protection except that one time. A pregnancy test confirmed my fears. I couldn't tell Mama. She would be so disappointed.

The only option was going somewhere to clear my head. Leaving town would give me an opportunity to think through things. After searching the Help Wanted ads I came across the perfect job opportunity. A traveling sales group.

I pitched the ideal to Mama without telling her why. She was extremely skeptical, but I was a young adult now. The decision was mine. She insisted on meeting the director and team leader, which they openly and willingly agreed to do.

Mama was very resourceful. All that was needed were names and a little information. Before long, she conducted a complete background check on the company and the adult leaders I would be traveling with. There would be about twenty of us in the group.

Apparently, my mother was satisfied with the results of her search. She strongly urged me not to hesitate to call if I was ready to come home.

My brother Dray was home from college for the summer. Before leaving, I told him the real reason for me going away. He swore to keep my secret, but I should have known he wouldn't. Dray didn't want me to leave home and insisted this was the time family was needed the most. In my mind, there was no choice. I kissed Mama and Dray goodbye and left, never mentioning a word to Karlos.

It was a good experience for me being on the road. Traveling from state to state, learning new things, and meeting some great people. Once the team learned about my experience driving trailers and assisting on long road trips with Mama, I became one of the lead drivers. That was awesome!

The best part of all was the friend I met named Mickey. She was several years older than me and also pregnant (about six months). We would talk until all hours at night about our situations. Finally, she asked me if my baby's father knew about the pregnancy.

I said, "No."

Mickey then asked, "Do you love him?"

My response was, "Very much."

She smiled and said, "Then you should tell him."

In my heart, I wanted to, but my mind feared rejection. If he were to ever tell me to get an abortion, I would be devastated.

My new friend just put her arms around me and said, "You have to take the risk. He has the right to know."

The next day, I decided she was right. My body was shaking like a limb on a tree. Mickey helped me dial the number. It seemed like the phone rung forever. Finally, Karlos' mom answered the phone. We chatted briefly before she called Karlos to pick up.

"Hello," he said, sounding nervous.

I tried to speak, but nothing would come out of my mouth until he said my name.

"Yeah, it's me," I said.

Karlos seemed to get excited and immediately began asking where I was. He took me off guard when, out of nowhere, he asked if I was pregnant.

"Huh?"

He said it a second time. "You're pregnant, aren't you?"

I said, "How did you know?"

Karlos laughed and said, "Because you always told me if you ever got pregnant, you would leave town and not tell me anything."

There was nervous laughter from both of us. I got up the nerve to ask the question. "What do you want me to do?"

"What do you want to do?" he responded.

After going back and forth several times, I just blurted out, "Do you want me to get an abortion?"

Again, he responded with a question, "Do you want to get an abortion?"

After a few times, Karlos finally said, "Yes, I want you to get an abortion."

Totally speechless, tears started rolling down my face and I couldn't breathe. Mickey snatched the phone and said, "What did you say to her? What did you say?" I reached over and hung up the phone.

Feeling defeated, rejected, humiliated, and unloved, again, I asked Mickey to help me find an abortion clinic. We went to our team leader who helped make the arrangements.

My heart became detached and I stopped feeling anything. The child I was carrying would always remind me about how the person I loved didn't love me back.

The next day, we went to that clinic. My friend just kept saying, "Are you sure? Are you sure? You're going to regret this if you're trying to get back at him."

"No," I said, "I'm sure."

After what seemed like hours, the nurse called my name. Without warning, I bolted out the front door. My mind was racing and everything inside me came pouring out as I vomited.

Mickey ran after me. All I heard was her saying, "You don't have to do this. Why don't you take a few days to think about it?"

I agreed and we returned to the hotel where I stayed for a couple days while the others went out to do sales calls. I fell into a deep depression, harboring so much anger toward Karlos but even more at myself for being so irresponsible.

It's ironic! Mama spent so much time protecting me from Brad, she never saw Karlos coming. One thing I knew for sure was that Brad may have been a liar and cheater but would never have asked me to get an abortion.

My state of mind was filled with so many unclear thoughts. I really wanted to call Mama. She would surely tell me to come home so we could work this out together.

I was struggling with tremendous shame and thoughts of terminating the pregnancy. It seemed any choice I made would be about my love or anger toward Karlos, not about right or wrong. Young, without family, scared, and confused! What a terrible position for anyone to be in.

Eventually, a decision was made that would further impact my mental stability for years to come. Aborting my child resulted in years of regrets. It was a decision I had to live with for the rest of my life. My emotions went from shame to guilt, stifling my ability to continue with the group. All I wanted was to go home and be with my mom.

It merely took a phone call, and she immediately purchased my one-way airplane ticket for me to return home.

After arriving home, we sat quietly for a while, which was extremely unusual. She was happy I was home but could tell something was wrong. My mom just kept saying how much she missed and loved me. It didn't stop the intense pain and deep depression that couldn't be shaken.

My mother was one of my best friends now, and I wanted her and Liz to know everything, but how? What would they think? Guilt prevented me from telling Liz although I knew she would have been nothing but supportive. Turns out, Mama already knew the horrible secret. Dray apparently told her during a discussion they had.

I was in deep thought when Mama said, "Baby, why didn't you tell me you were pregnant?"

The expression on my face spoke for itself. She smiled and didn't wait for my response before asking another question. "I'm your mother no matter what. You know that, don't you?"

Nodding my head yes, the only words were, "I lost the baby."

Tears streamed down Mama's face as she said, "I would like to have met my grandchild. Don't ever be so ashamed of anything that you feel you're better off with strangers than with your family who loves you."

Her words sent me into a crying fit. I knew then she could never know about the abortion. I believed Mama would never forgive me. More importantly, I wholeheartedly believed this was something that not even God would forgive me for.

There was no desire to even hear about church, let alone attend one. I was convinced by religion that God wouldn't want anything to do with someone like me. Building a closer relationship was completely out of the question. There was so much darkness all around me.

Dray saw how depressed I was and wanted to lift my spirit. He convinced me to go out dancing and have a little fun. We went to a popular club in the area. I was having a good time when one of Karlos' sisters, Nancy, walked into the club. Out of all the places she could have gone to in the city, Nancy chose that club on that night. She spotted us right away and came over to say hello, which turned into a whole evening of good conversation.

Karlos and I had not communicated since we talked on the phone. He had no idea I was back home. It was apparent Karlos hadn't mentioned anything about my condition to his sister, so neither did I.

As we wrapped up the night, Nancy made it a point of stating she'd be sure to let her brother know we bumped into each other.

At the time, I could care less what she told Karlos. There was a strong dislike, teetering on hatred, toward him. It wouldn't have bothered me one bit if we never spoke again.

No such luck! After seeing Nancy, I had to speak with Karlos to get some type of closure. reaching out to him wasn't easy. My hands started shaking as I dialed his number.

Just as I was about to hang up, Karlos answered the phone. We exchanged brief pleasantries before agreeing to meet and talk. My only thought was to show no signs of weakness or hurt. There would be no crying!

When the day arrived, I tried to hide every feeling behind my smile. Initially we had small talk before getting to the question about my current condition. The answer was short and sweet without explanation, "I lost the baby!"

I couldn't admit to myself, let alone anybody else, what I had done; so from that day to this, Karlos never knew the pregnancy was terminated.

"Why didn't you call me back after hanging up?" He asked.

I bluntly exclaimed, "For what? You left me out there by myself."

All I remember him saying was something about being scared and he didn't know what to do. So much for showing no emotions.

My anger was boiling over as I yelled, "You were scared? What about me? I was without my family and friends. We always talked about the what-if. Abortion was never supposed to be an option!"

Then the truth came to light. Karlos blamed a conversation he had with Julian on his doubts about whether the baby was his. It was also the reason he refused to say the words *I love you*.

While I thought everything was cool between me and Julian, he was leading my boyfriend to believe we were more than friends. Karlos was so naive. He couldn't see how jealous Julian was, and he (Julian) would've said anything to break us up. Well, it worked.

Karlos was supposed to love me, but he didn't. That was the ultimate betrayal, and for a long time, I wanted nothing but revenge. Another person that needed to be hurt the way he dished it out.

In a twisted kind of way, I wasn't that angry at Julian. His actions were provoked by how he felt about me. Karlos had no excuse.

My attitude and disposition about relationships became very cynical. I withheld any affection and began putting up walls as soon as someone tried to get close. I refused to be completely broken… ever again. Broken by toxic relationships.

Choices

Choices! If only the hands of time could go back to the
moment of innocence.
A time before dark nights and virtue lost.
How I long for the silly days of old.
Before pressures of life grabbed hold and led down
some bumpy and uncertain highways.

Choices! The roads we took were not meant to be our last stop.
Dead ends and barricades seemed to block destiny's plan.
Graveled lanes leaving invisible scars meant to bruise the
very core of our being.
Ahhh! The choices we made to taste freedom's mere existence

Choices! Wisdom was not allowed to be our friend.
The voice of her guidance was kept at bay.
Blinded by the storms of desire. Unable to see the
Danger signs ahead.
Running towards the slippery slope of young love.
How the residue of its lasting grip leaves
us with much to be said.

Choices! We can never right the wrongs of what was,
or what could have been.
Let us push forward. Ahead towards a new journey.
Our intended destination was never blocked, only detoured.
Spring forth! The choices of yesterday don't
define who we are today.
Our final destiny awaits the arrival of soldiers.
Kings and queens in our own right.

What do I choose?
I choose to love despite the pain it may cause.
I choose to forgive instead of seek vindication.
I elect to break the bondage of guilt and shame.
What do I choose? I choose you!
I lift up the royal blood running through your veins.
Let go of the past and choose to wear your crown.

Choices!

Chapter 12

Daybreak

As much as I wanted to hate Karlos, something inside me wouldn't allow it. Don't misunderstand the facts, I was still angry, but it was slowly subsiding. I realized it wasn't a thin line between love and hate but a war between love and hurt. The latter won out and was the dominate source of my pain.

People say that in due time, the pain will go away. Well time didn't heal all wounds for me. It did allow some of the wounds to close while the scars remained. That's the price of not loving myself first. Not understanding that some relationships were only meant to be friendships.

I regret ever crossing the line of friendship because that's something, once destroyed, is very difficult to regain. It was valued above all. Eventually we tried getting back to our plutonic friendship, but it was never the same. Trust was destroyed and he was too afraid it would only lead to him getting hurt. He was right and I needed to move on.

If only it were that simple. We shared something that could never be changed—conception of a child! No matter how much I tried to forget about it, the fact remained that my body held an unborn child. Guilt continued to eat at me with the constant thoughts of what-if. What if Karlos had not said those words? What if he had been happy? What if Mama knew about the abortion? What if the child I carried was my only son? What if? The *what-ifs* were extremely overwhelming.

I had to concentrate on something more productive before the pain completely took control of me. It was time to get back on track with a brighter future.

First, Some distance had to be put between me and Karlos, so I reenrolled into a larger higher education institution. It was about sixty miles from where we lived.

Going to a large university in another city was the perfect opportunity to provide the necessary space. It was close enough to visit with Mama regularly but far enough to help me get over yet another painful experience.

My first semester was hard. The campus seemed enormous. Likely because I was accustomed to small private school settings. Primarily with small class sizes and easy access to instructors. Even the classes at the community college were more intimate. The large auditorium style courses took some getting used too. However, I quickly found out the campus was smaller than some other universities in Michigan.

I ended up living on campus my first year there. What an experience! The suite slept four (4) with two people in each bedroom. The two suites were separated by the common area, including a bathroom. The bedrooms had enough space to fit two twin-size beds and two dressers comfortably.

This was one of the worst living arrangements of my life. My immediate roommate was the complete opposite of me. One of my suitemates was an artist. She got a bum deal getting stuck with someone who could care less about cleanliness. It didn't take long for me to move out of the dorms into a campus apartment by myself. That was the best decision I could have made at that time.

Also, during my first year, I connected with a small group of like-minded friends. There was Harry, Rosita, Dywan, Willie, Bridgette, Elgin, Ed, Laverne, Andre, and Charlotte (Co-Co).

Harry and I became bonded right away and were like brother and sister. It was through him that I met Sue. She and Harry began dating around my second or third year at the school. Sue didn't seem to like me much at first because Harry and I were extremely close. What she didn't know at the time was that we were siblings and just happened to have different parents. We understood each other and had a lot in common.

No worries, I quickly grew on her with my hilarious personality, fighting spirit, and no-nonsense disposition. She had such a sweet spirit, and it would anger me when bullies wanted to take advantage or challenge her. I was always ready to *ride down* on some cowards, as she would always say.

After a while, we became a funny trio. There were times when we'd be together, and I would introduce one of them as my best friend. Before the other could be introduced, I would be humorously corrected. Yes! I learned to always present them both at the same time as my best friends, Harry and Sue. I loved them both.

Let's get back to my like-minded friends. Our small group became very close and decided to come up with a name to identify ourselves. We ended up with Renegades. Beats me how we came up with the name, but it stuck. At some point, we became very serious about humanity and did some really good things.

We were passionate and always looking for opportunities to have a voice on campus. The topic of reestablishing the local NAACP came up.

"Why don't we start our own chapter?" Someone exclaimed.

"Yeah, let's do that," I lightheartedly commented.

Rosita was quick to blurt out, "Let's nominate Cornbread (my nickname) as president."

"I second that," someone else yelled out.

Before long, it was unanimously decided.

The look on my face must have been priceless because the room roared with laughter.

"What! I don't know nothing about organizing no NAACP chapter, I protested!"

To get the heat off me, I shot back, "Harry can be the president."

He quickly declined and said, "I'll be the vice president."

I was laughing so hard my next words were difficult to get out. "Why do I have to be the president?"

Bridgette sassily said, "Because you're a leader, Cornbread. You can do it."

A leader! That was news to me. I wouldn't even know where to begin.

What started out as a joke, became a serious discussion. I still don't know how they convinced me to take on such a big task. Somehow, we put the gears in motion and formally got recognized as an active chapter of the NAACP.

Passion, friendship, and desire were our primary motivation to make a difference. We needed to identify a specific focus. After agreeing on an international cause, the chapter began organizing an anti-apartheid march. The sole purpose was to convince universities, businesses, and others to divest out of South Africa. Simply put, Apartheid supported racial segregation and oppression against non-white citizens.

We spent time becoming familiar and acquainted with faculty, fraternities, sororities, and other organizations on campus in preparation for the march. I don't recall a single person saying no, and the word spread like wildfire. After much research, flyers were disseminated to explain the state of South Africa. Everyone needed to know our rationale for asking the university to divest.

The primary colors to be worn for the march were red and black clothing. Red ribbons would also be passed out to tie around the arm. Red represented the blood, and black represented the people.

Before long, various departments at the university asked what they could do to help. Our Response was "whatever support you're able to provide."

The art department made a casket and painted it black. This was to represent those who died, and others being oppressed. The design also included handles on each side for easy transport during the march. Numerous male students volunteered to carry the casket. A local funeral home offered their hearse to lead the demonstration.

Wow! students wanted to purchase flowers. Fraternities, sororities, faculty, and various groups on campus made banners and signs. The media was contacted, and they committed to covering the event.

Things were going so perfectly it was exciting and frightening at the same time. Here were some young adults born and raised in multiple urban cities. There was a stigma, which often caused people to negatively view groups based on their color and/or the communities where they lived.

Unfortunately, many of the folks who believed the stereotypes about people of color from urban cities didn't have a clue. They thought we were all uneducated and violent. Many of them had no personal knowledge or relationships with anyone who lived there.

Can anything good come from Detroit, Saginaw, Flint or any inner city? Look what our villages produced. Leaders! We were preparing for a life-changing event.

The closer it got to the date of the march, the more our nerves were trying to get the best of us. Had we forgotten anything? Did we notify everyone? Was there too much of this or not enough of that?

Everything seemed to be going smoothly until a few days before the event. We learned another larger university decided to organize a march on the exact same date and time. The media opted to cover the other college. Discouragement was quickly invading the team, including me.

Just as anger started becoming contagious, a scary calm came over me. I heard a voice say, "Move forward."

This was about a cause much greater than us. The primary purpose was focused on *divestment*. The success or failure of the march was not only about blacks in South Africa. It was about global oppression against black and brown people at universities, in our communities, and across the world.

I realized and accepted we had something more powerful than the media. The ear of God! All this time believing my Father was angry with me. He was just watching and waiting to hear my voice.

I asked God for nothing less than victory. That is exactly what he gave us. The event was more than successful as thousands of students, faculty, and even residents joined us along the route.

A valuable lesson was learned that day. Faith defined the difference between my source and resource. Belief that God would hear me was my source, the media was only a resource. I never stopped believing in God. I thought he stopped believing in me.

After the march, our organization grew from a small group of silly friends to more members than I can recall. Until this very day, many in our group keep in touch and frequently reminisce about the old days. Some became life-long friends, while others went in their own direction. But I'm sure they, too, have fond memories.

It was great! coming to the realization that I had the gift to lead and inspire others.

The victory didn't end there. It led to another cause that would shed light on why so many people were sharing their tragedies and trauma with me. While child molestation was always a burden, it would become my purpose.

There came a time when one of my classes required me to write a paper with specific research and data collection criteria. The instructor provided a list of topics to choose from. It had to be something that conflicted with many religious doctrines. I wanted to do something that would have a positive impact on others while addressing childhood sexual abuse. The topic that most conflicted with my Christian faith dealt with what was then called alternative lifestyles.

I remembered a girl from my neighborhood who was openly gay. Back then this term was broadly defined for an entire population of people. Today, the community would be better identified as lesbian, gay, bisexual, transgender and questioning (LGBTQ). There are other identifiers that have emerged but are not included in this book.

It stumped me as to why! She was very attractive and had no problems getting attention from males. Goes to show how ignorant I was, not knowing appearance had nothing to do with sexuality.

I later learned she was exposed to severe early childhood sexual abuse by a male and female friend of the family. I wanted to learn more about whether there was a strong correlation between childhood sexual abuse and lifestyle choices. Specifically as it related to women. The point was not to neglect males, but in order to identify a manageable target population, I focused only on females.

How was I going to accomplish this? It would require finding a way to interview women that openly identified themselves. They likely wouldn't believe a heterosexual woman would be interested in conducting such a research study. It seemed this was an impossible task and I'd bitten off more than I could chew.

Before giving up, I turned to my friends. Rosita mentioned a young lady named Tora that we've seen from time to time. "She typically hangs out at the intramural building playing basketball," Rosita stated. "It wouldn't hurt to ask her for help."

"Do you know her personally," I inquired?

Rosita laughed and said, "No, but I know she identifies as gay."

"Well, that's a lot of help," I responded. "Am I just supposed to walk up to her and say, hey, I heard you're gay, can you help me out?"

Again, Rosita snickered and said, "Not quite like that."

I had no clue what my approach would be until the moment it happened. The opportunity finally presented itself. I was taking a break in the gym when Tora walked in and sat down. I did a little self-encouragement and thought to myself, It's now or never!

Here goes! "Excuse me, my name is Bree, but a lot of my friends call me cornbread."

She replied, "Oh hi, my name is Tora. What kind of name is Cornbread?"

"It's a nickname because of my love for cornbread. Hot water bread, skillet, oven baked, crackling, whatever way my mom cooks it."

"That's pretty cool," she said.

After a few more pleasantries, it felt like I was about to make a fool of myself. However, my drive to complete the assignment caused me to press forward.

"Tora, it's nice to meet you. This is going to sound strange. It might even make you think about walking away, but please hear me out. I have a friend that thought you'd be a good person to speak with. I'm required to conduct a comprehensive research study for a class."

I went on to discuss requirements in detail as Tora listened intently. After explaining the project in its entirety, I asked, "Would you be willing to participate and answer a few questions?" Tora was intrigued and agreed.

Tora smiled and said, "I'll be your test subject. Go ahead."

She completed the necessary release forms before proceeding with some opening questions. We later moved into more sensitive areas of discussion.

"The next question is very personal in nature," I said. How do you identify when it comes to sexual preference/orientation?"

It immediately broke the tension as she chuckled, "How does it look like I identify? Isn't it obvious? I'm gay!"

"Well considering I don't know if being gay has a specific look, that would be a no. It's not obvious," I lightheartedly joked.

"That's true," Tora confessed. "You can't really look at someone and know their preference or how they identify." We both agreed, then moved on through a series of delicate questions.

"Wow Cornbread," Tora said. "That was good. Some of the questions really made me dig deep. I mean truly thought provoking."

Yes! That was the perfect response. "I'm glad you found it useful. I'm hoping you can help me recruit other women that might be willing to participate in the research?"

Tora was so impressed, she jumped into action and arranged interviews with fifteen other women. The agreement was she would be my forerunner to explain the project to each participant before introducing my role. I would take it from there.

All of the participants that were interviewed identified as either gay or Lesbian. Fourteen out of fifteen admitted to being exposed to some form of childhood sexual abuse. Some by men, some by women, and others by both.

This is not to say that everyone in the LGBTQ community were exposed to childhood sexual abuse. It just means that about ninety-three percent of the people in my sample had, which is greater than the national average.

Participants disclosed that their abusers were known to them; hence, the word *stranger danger* can be misleading and overrepresented. We must also become comfortable about discussing *familial danger*.

This was not just a research study. Without knowing it at the time, I was ministering to these women. Assisting some, who asked for help, with seeking counseling and other supportive services. They were looking to heal from childhood trauma. Some of them had never talked about the sexual abuse and realized there was still an open wound.

The research concluded that childhood sexual abuse had a strong probability of shaping participant's views about self-identity and sexualization. The research included recordings, personal statements, waivers, releases, etc., and earned me an A+ in the class.

My instructor kept the materials to use as an example for other classes. She strongly urged me to go into social work because of my ability to engage others about sensitive subject matters. That's exactly what I did, quickly switching my major from computer science.

This study taught me an important lesson. It's not my job to judge anyone, nor is it yours! That's God's job. He doesn't require any help. Jesus commanded us to love. I don't recall scripture saying except when—. We can love without foregoing our purpose and calling. What would Jesus do?

I must have drawn many with love. Somehow the word spread quickly. Not so much about the research study but more about how people felt supported and heard. The floodgates were open, leading to a very diverse group of people seeking my assistance.

Initially, my purpose was to complete a class assignment, but it turned out to be much more. It seemed that survivors of sexual abuse across campus, males and females, started reaching out. Revealing their stories and just wanting someone to talk to. Secrets they had not disclosed to anyone.

I also had friends who, one by one, began divulging childhood sexual abuse. Unspeakable acts by fathers, uncles, cousins, aunts, siblings, and family friends that left them broken as a person. Many struggled with severe mental health conditions.

After all this time, I realized my purpose. I knew that God was using me to help others heal. Imagine that! *Choosing someone like me.* Strict religious teachings had me believing God had no purpose for a person with my background. There were many scriptures inaccurately referenced that tried to guilt me and others into submission to Christ.

That's not how God operates. He gives us freedom of choice. We're not forced to do anything. How genuine would our walk be if submission only occurred from fear of judgement by man.

Think about how you've felt when others had the tendency to judge you. Whether it's because you looked or acted differently. They came to a conclusion because you didn't conform to their way of thinking, dressing, speaking, etc.

Let's say your decision is to adapt because you don't want to stand out as being different. Your heart and mind are not fully present in the conformity. It takes a lot of energy and mental capacity to keep up the pretense. You eventually give up and revert back to your old way of doing things. This would be considered coerced conformity. It is temporary and not a long-term solution.

I believe my college experience was a turning point. What outcome might have occurred if I pre-judged those women? What opportunity would have been missed?

A powerful ministry was revealed. While it became a great passion, there would be many obstacles to overcome. Darker days were waiting to detour me from this thing I was feeling strongly about. But for now, the breaking of the day was near. It was beautiful and within my reach.

Daybreak

My tomorrow started today. The darkness of my past keeps trying
to pull me down, but the sun is rising and daybreak is near.
Midnight is disappearing and I reach to embrace the daylight.
Day, come now, for I fear you will pass me by too quickly.
Midnight tries to expand its territory in my being, but
light and dark cannot occupy the same space.

The fear of midnight tries to immobilize my steps, but I
keep reaching, I'm reaching and reaching for daylight.
I can't give up! I won't give up!
Midnight wants me to believe I'm mediocre,
but daylight commands my excellence.
Midnight named me unattractive, but daylight rebukes
the voice of darkness and calls me beautiful.
Every inch, every curve, every flaw, from the top of my head
to the bottom of my feet, is daylight. Darkness you have
no power over me. My sense of being is not determined by
who you say I am but who I'm called to be. My mind, my
mind is growing stronger every day. Step back, Midnight,
I slam the door in your face. I'm out! Deuces!
I'm running toward the *Light*.

Chapter 13

Wake Up, Li'l Bruthas

It seemed things were looking up. The tragedies in my life were being used to help others be delivered from pain. It wasn't about being super religious, quoting scriptures or even talking about the Bible. There was still a lot of mistrust and skepticism about the church overall. I strongly believed in the Godhead but had little trust in the people or institutions.

A big part of me felt fellowship was necessary. The other part was tainted because of traumatic experiences I witnessed by those who professed to represent the church. People like Bill and others were causing harm. Often killing the spirit of innocent children, new believers and those seeking to be healed.

Despite my skepticism, I was still being guided by something more powerful than I'd ever felt before. An evolution was occurring. I had a way to positively redirect pent-up anger. Even Mama was overjoyed with my new-found passion.

My relationship with Mama was nothing short of amazing. We were always having lunch, dinner, or hanging out somewhere. She'd pick me up from my campus apartment, or I would drive home for the weekend and we'd just go. Nothing really planned, just an opportunity for us to get together. Interesting how things changed once I became a young adult. We could talk about anything from school performance to dating.

While sitting at the kitchen table talking to Mama and listening to her laugh, I decided it was time to tell her about Bill and Rocky. However, that would have to wait until our next outing. At the moment, I was enjoying our latest conversation about her beautiful garden.

My mom was always into urban gardening and grew fresh vegetables, which tasted much better than store-bought products. I never understood how the term *urban gardening* was credited to suburbanites. They came into the city to plant gardens and received credit for discovering something that was already there. Sounds like another Cristobal Colon (aka Christopher Columbus) story.

Mama really enjoyed being in her garden and could be found there at any given time. She was also active in volunteerism and did a lot in the community. Mama was most passionate about children and helping others. Wondered where I got that from!

There came a time when one of my mother's fishing buddies became sick. She made it her business to establish a daily routine of visiting her at the hospital. It was good to see my mom keeping active.

Although Mama seemed very busy, she always arranged for us to spend time together, and was glad to hear that my grades had significantly improved. This was crucial as I was about to enter my senior year of under-grad. She was also excited about my new job.

As my junior year was coming to an end, I got a position working with an organization that provided independent living services to adults with disabilities. Mama thought it was great. That was the last conversation we had.

While working in the main office, I suddenly began to feel sharp stabbing discomfort in my chest. The pain quickly became intense. My boss, Cappy, heard me yelling. She came running into the room and wanted to call 911. I insisted on going home because the visions in my head was showing me something horrible.

Cappy didn't understand but there was no time to explain how or why I knew Mama was in trouble. She would likely not believe me anyway.

Outside of me providing directions to my house, we rode in complete silence. Cappy looked extremely concerned but I couldn't talk. I just needed to concentrate on what I was clearly seeing in my head.

We pulled up to the house where my brother Dray was waiting at the door. I jumped out the car yelling, "Where is Mama?"

He looked confused, and I yelled again, "Where is Mama?"

Dray said, "She went to visit at the hospital."

"How long has she been gone?" I said.

"I don't know. Why? What's wrong?" Dray asked.

By this time, I was hysterical.

Dray thanked my boss and coworker then escorted me in the house to try and get clarity. The one thing he heard was that Mama's in trouble. We have to go find her.

Eventually, Dray realized he had to calm my hysteria before we could do anything. He provided something that caused me to fall asleep for a while. I woke up to my brother shaking me, saying, "Let's go look for Mama. It's dark and she's not home yet."

My mother was very scheduled, so this must have been a red flag for Dray.

After quickly grabbing everything needed, panic set in again. I jumped in the passenger side of the car, and Dray drove, asking me which way to go.

"Turn here, go straight, turn right." I was a human navigation system.

It felt like Mama was getting weaker, and we were losing her. She was somewhere close. I just couldn't narrow down the exact location.

As it got later, we had to give up the search with plans to get up early the next day to resume.

The next day seemed like it took forever to arrive. At first light, Dray and I jumped in the car and began circling one particular community, but I couldn't feel Mama anymore. I knew she was gone.

We filed a missing person's report, and the waiting nearly killed us. My mother never came home that night or any night thereafter.

I contacted a good friend of mine, Jay, who happened to be over the homicide division of our local police department. A description of the area was given to let him know where I thought Mama was and what we suspected. He immediately jumped into action, and my suspicions were correct. A couple days following my call to Jay, two children were playing in a backyard when they stumbled across the body of a female corpse. It was the exact area we had been circling.

When Jay contacted me, the sound of his voice trembling was all I needed to hear. Mama was unrecognizable as the heat had caused rapid decomposition, but he was pretty sure it was her.

My uncle went to the city morgue to identify her body based on certain identifying characteristics. Uncle Bob was cautioned not to bring me and Dray as it would only make a painful situation worse.

There was nothing anyone could say to comfort us. Waiting for my uncle to return home was the worst day of our lives. When he walked through the door, no words had to be spoken. It was Mama.

This time, there was no one standing at the doors, so I ran. With all my might, I ran. My brother bolted out the door after me. It was even a difficult task for him to catch me. He was a track star with various first place medals.

I couldn't hear, couldn't see, and could barely breathe, but I ran until Dray finally caught up. Everything was quite a blur after that.

There was nothing but darkness. Daybreak disappeared and Midnight won. A war between good and evil was ripping me apart.

Dray tried to be strong for me, but I could tell it was killing him inside. He and Mama were always very close. His whole goal in life was to get rich and take care of her.

Planning my mother's funeral must have been a nightmare for Dray. How could anyone concentrate on obituaries, funeral arrangements, cost or anything else. Somehow, he fought his way through it. I hardly remember being involved. Dray and Uncle Bob took care of most things.

As for me, I sunk so deep into a depressive state, it was doubtful I'd ever recover. This was one tragedy my mind was not strong enough to handle.

I'm not sure how Karlos found out, but I likely called. I remember him showing up at Mama's house. It escapes me as to what we talked about, if anything. What I do recall is him saying he'd be there for me.

Unfortunately, that promise was short-lived. I didn't see or hear much from him after that day for a long time. There's also no recollection of him attending Mama's funeral. To be honest, I wouldn't have remembered even if he did.

Eventually, I stopped caring about anyone or anything other than my brother and those closest to me. Seems I had finally broken. My mind, body, and spirit. What use to be a *good life* quickly began spiraling down, and I couldn't stop what started happening. It was like an out-of-body experience as I watched myself become uncaged.

Dray and I struggled for a long time to overcome the pain of Mama's murder. The man who killed her was the son of a church member, and our families knew each other well.

The criminal trial revealed he was a long-time substance abuser. Somehow, he didn't get convicted for first degree murder because premeditation couldn't be proven. How is it not premeditation when you monitor a person's schedule, follow them, ask for a ride home, and ask to stop at a store where you have friends waiting to attack her?

He was convicted of second-degree murder with life instead of mandatory life. Eligible for parole after twelve years. Over my dead body will he get out in twelve years, I promised myself. I'll be involved with every parole hearing to assure he rots behind bars. The command to love was no longer in my heart.

Fury was the only word that could describe the way I felt. He was going to have the privilege of living with three meals, a cot, and few worries. Dray and I had to wade through the mess of confusion and anger we both felt. The only thing I could hope for was a violent assault on him as true punishment.

I knew the teachings about Christ turning the other cheek and all, but I wasn't Christ and had no intentions on turning the other cheek.

Most people couldn't tell how self-destructive I really was. Wearing a mask of smiles allowed me to function in my depressed state. There was an invisible wall shielded by a composed demeanor. No one ever knew what was going on in my mind or when I would become unhinged.

There were little things that set me off into a rage one moment, and a quiet calm the next. The eye of the storm had returned. What seemed nice and serene would quickly become a violent tornado, destroying everything in its path.

There was so much hatred fueling my very existence. Trust no one, expect the worse of everyone. That was my motto. I was broken, angry, resentful, and destructive.

Partying became my routine from the time I got off work on Friday all the way through Sunday. If there was music and drinks, I was there. Usually with someone appointed as my designated driver. It didn't matter that my body was unable to handle the effects of alcohol and made me violently sick. I wanted something, anything, that would stop the pain.

I knew all the after-hour spots and the places to go following the after hour. My body was a mere shell of a human being as I functioned robotically.

There was a yearning to hurt the man that caused my family so much pain. He didn't deserve to live, not even with his freedom taken away. Why didn't Michigan have the death penalty?

This tragedy warranted an eye for an eye, tooth for tooth, limb for limb, and life for life. My mind kept asking what my mouth couldn't say. What kind of God would allow so much pain where innocent people suffer while the guilty seem to prosper?

I might as well live life on my own terms and get mine for me and my brother.

Dray and I were both trying to cope with our pain and didn't conversate much about what we were each going through. He threw himself into work, traveling and being the financial provider he was trained to be.

Mama, Grandpa, and Uncle Bob taught my brothers if anything ever happened to them, they were to look out for me. That's exactly what Dray did. Always trying to make sure things were okay, but he needed looking after too.

We clung to each other for dear life and became closer than ever. There was nothing we wouldn't do for each other.

I specifically recall one birthday, Dray wanted to buy me a surprise gift. He knew I wasn't big on celebrating my birthday due to the timing of Tony's death. He went to one of my favorite stores to scout out the perfect outfits but didn't really know the right size. What he did know, was I had lost a lot of weight and could fit into his jeans which were just a little snug because of my hips.

Do you know what he did? Something that only a brother who truly loved his sister could or would do. Dray was really silly and asked the salesclerks if he could try on one of the dresses for his sister who was about his size.

Now you know those salesclerks didn't believe a word of that story. Nonetheless, they allowed him to try on the outfits. He ended up purchasing all items. Dray tried to convince them that he really did have a sister who was almost his twin. I don't think he was very convincing.

My birthday arrived and Dray surprised me with some awesome outfits, but one of the dresses did not fall quite right. He gave me the gift receipt so I could exchange it if necessary.

Needless to say, after showing up at the store and explaining my reason for the return, they gave me their full attention. I began telling them how one of the dresses didn't fit quite right. The entire staff was amazed and burst out laughing saying, "He really does have a sister."

Dray had already told me the story, so I wasn't surprised by their reaction, and assured them that I was all woman, and my brother was all man.

Everyone had a good laugh about the whole situation, and then one of the girls asked for my brother's number saying, "That's the kind of man I want. He really loves you. My brother would never have done something like that for me."

"That's my brother," I proudly responded.

She was never provided with his number because he was already in a serious relationship. As for me, there were moments like this that I really felt alive, but most of the time, I was barely existing.

I dropped out of school and my purpose was no longer important. The words of prayer had departed from my lips. I became cold as ice and found myself getting into silly confrontations, daring people to cross me.

It got to the point that although we had a beautiful home, I rarely lived in it. Sleeping wherever I laid my head and not really caring what dangers were lurking around the corner.

There was a lack of emotion and drive which led to me hanging around people I didn't really have anything in common with. This included Pete.

Pete was a business owner in the community who was known for his no-nonsense personality and serious demeanor. Most people were afraid of him, because he presented with a tough guy attitude, but not me. I'd been in his company many times. I was observant but had very little to say.

Our first verbal interaction occurred when he was scolding his best friend, AD, for a statement Pete felt was incorrect. I must have been staring at him because the next thing I knew, Pete angrily asked me what I was looking at.

Without thinking, in an uncaring, nasty, and unfearful manner, I said "You, which ain't much."

Everyone in the room looked like they were ready to run for cover. I just sat there and stared him down without blinking, silently daring the bully to make a move toward me.

My heart lacked fear and everybody knew I wasn't afraid to respond to a threat of harm.

After several seconds of silence, there was a need to defuse the obvious tension building in the room. I began explaining why AD was correct in his statements.

Pete was visibly impressed and asked AD, "Why couldn't you just explain it like that?"

This time, without looking up at him, I sarcastically retorted, "Because he ain't me."

I had a half smile on my face. Pete laughed and apparently it gave everyone else permission to laugh. This caused me to discontinue my half-hearted smile. There was no way I was going to let anybody control me like that.

It felt likely that Pete and I would be natural enemies because I didn't fear him. The exact opposite happened. He was captivated by my lack of concern and quick comebacks. Pete also saw I wasn't chasing after him like a lot of other women. It's probably why he pursued me.

We ended up becoming a hot item from that day until he *loved* me enough to send me home.

AD, his girlfriend (Abby), Pete, and I began spending a lot of time together. Abby and I were talking during one of our weekend gatherings. As Pete and AD were exiting the room she leaned over and whispered, "I need to talk to you."

I slid closer and Abby started saying Pete was in love with me. She'd never seen him as relaxed around anybody like he was with me.

"There's something special about you," she said.

Abby continued, "Pete says you have a sweet spirit and different than the other *chicks* he's dated. You're smarter than him (Abby laughed) and he likes that. Pete just don't wanna hurt you or be the reason you get hurt."

"What are you talkin' bout? Me getting hurt?" I snapped.

"Pete's got a lot of women tryin' to get at him, and they'll do whatever it takes for his attention. I've never seen him fight this hard to be a one woman's man."

"Is that right?" I asked

"Yeah girl. You done made the man soft. He's happy when you're around and misses you when you're not. AD and I ain't never seen him like this before."

Abby went on to say how Pete was more concerned about me than he was about himself. She continued by telling me about his homicidal ex-girlfriend.

"That woman ain't working with a full deck, if you know what I mean," Abby joked. "She's caused problems whenever he gets into a new relationship."

It felt good to know that a man loved me so much. I wasn't in love with him but was appreciative that someone made me feel safe and wanted to provide protection. I was going to have his back no matter what.

Just then, Pete and AD walked back into the room. "What you two in here talkin' bout?" Pete asked.

"What else but you," I responded in a teasing voice.

"Yeah, it figures," he said.

We all laughed and spent the rest of the evening playing cards and telling jokes.

Later that night, I could tell Pete was deeply troubled by something and asked him to share it. He looked at me with tears in his eyes. I was shocked because crying was not his thing.

He said, "It's time for you to go home."

My immediate response was, "No! We gonna ride or die... together."

Pete said, "That's what I'm afraid of. What man wouldn't want a ride or die woman? I don't want you to get hurt because of me, and right now, you're my weakness. These chicks out hear are silly and I could never live with myself if anything ever happened to you."

Tears were uncontrollably streaming down his face like a water faucet. I couldn't help but cry with and for him.

Pete could barely get the words out but pulled himself together enough to say, "I had a dream that scared me, and I believe it was God speaking to me. You have to go home."

"What? Really? What's God got to do with this!" I yelled.

Pete looked at me so sadly and said, "I knew you were special from day one. As long as you're here, I'm putting you at risk. I'm not asking you to go home, I'm telling you. I may go to hell for a lot of stuff but bringing harm on you ain't one of 'em."

I wanted to be angry but couldn't because it was only out of his concern for my well being.

The next day, I packed all my things, and Pete took me home. Back to an empty dark shell of a place where my brother and I coexisted.

Dray was always traveling and never knew how I was dying inside. He was probably experiencing a little darkness of his own, which is why he stayed away so much. Always making sure there was enough money to pay bills and get some of the things I wanted, not really knowing about my life with Pete.

A couple months after Pete took me home he was killed. I don't know the whole story but heard it was investigated as a homicide. There was some suspicion that his ex-girlfriend was involved. It's also when Abby told me the true story behind Pete's decision. He received multiple threats about getting rid of me, or else.

I was completely distraught and so tired of losing people. There was daddy, Aunt Sarah, Grandpa, Tony, Mama, and now Pete.

I wanted so desperately to talk to either one of my best friends, Sue, Harry, or Liz but didn't want to burden them as they were each trying to live their own lives. This was just in my own mind because I'm positive that neither of them would have thought it was a burden. They would have quickly responded without a second thought. It was my own pride that kept me from reaching out for help.

Although I couldn't admit it at the time, God saw my pain and the dark place my soul was in. Since my pride stopped me from seeking the help I needed, He sent my good friend Risa. She planted herself in our lives like a deep-rooted tree and refused to be plucked up.

I came to trust that no matter the day or hour, if Dray or I called, she came without hesitation. Sometimes risking her own safety to pull me out of whatever mess I had gotten into. Unfortunately, it still wasn't enough to shake me out of my depressed state of mind.

Eventually it became so unbearable my only solution was to stop the pain. I drove my Dodge Shelby to a major street, parked it in the middle turn lane, a distance away from the stop lights, and waited.

Things seemed to move in slow motion. I waited for the light to change and cars to pick up enough speed before walking into ongoing traffic with my eyes closed. I could barely hear the horns blowing or screeching tires. The wind from cars moving past me was strong, but I refused to open my eyes.

At last, it must be over. There was complete silence. Nothing until I heard a woman yelling, "Are you all right?"

I opened my eyes, and a woman was standing there saying, "You're special, and it's not your time. There's too much work to do. It's not your time!" she just kept saying. "It's not your time."

Out of nowhere, there was a crowd of people forming around me. Up until that point, I didn't realize I was on my knees.

Looking around I asked, "Where is the woman?"

People asked, "What woman?"

"The woman that was just talking to me," I exclaimed.

No one in the crowd saw the woman. They just kept saying how lucky I was.

"Not a single car hit you. It's as if there was a barrier around you," somebody shouted.

One person started saying how crazy it was because at least one of the cars should have hit me. I was helped to my feet. Someone called the police, but they never showed up even though we were just down the street from the police station.

A man in the crowd asked if I were trying to hurt myself. My response was that I took some medication that had me out of it (I lied).

When the police didn't show up, an older couple made sure I got back to my car safely. They provided me with their contact information in case there was a need to talk. I thanked them and drove away still feeling like I wanted to die.

My only thought was, why didn't God just let me die. It didn't seem like my life was worth much anyway.

What did that woman mean by *it's not my time*? Why did her voice sound so familiar, and who was she to tell me about my life?

I became preoccupied with the woman that no one seemed to see. Then it hit me. It was the voice that spoke when Rocky tried to rape me and when I almost hurt Mama.

A miracle had just occurred, but I still wasn't ready to let go of my anger. It comforted me for a long time.

Wake Up, Li'l Bruthas

Wake up, li'l bruthas!
Stop running! Turn around and look at what's coming at you.
An army called fear and soldiers with you in their view.
The war ain't on drugs, but the battle is against you.
Suddenly opioid is a crisis, while crack and
heroin's destructive path never ends.
Death is chasing you, and time ain't your friend.
Hidden messages are in motion, and your mind is under attack.
Wake up, li'l bruthas! The label of criminal
has a target on your back.
Don't you know that the prisons are waiting for your arrival?
The world ain't caring 'bout your mental health
past or your struggle for survival.

Who are you? You're the sons of kings and queens.
You are wise fathers from whom your sons can glean.
Bruthas of strength, sons of beauty, and husbands of blackness.
You are lions at heart, friends to courage, don't accept anything less.
You are the trumpet sounding the alarm of urgency.
It goes deep into the waters of our ancestor's
blood that stretches far and wide.
Too many have given their blood. Too
many have sacrificed and died.

It's time to step into your rightful position.
You are not a product of your environment
or a slave to your condition.

You and your seed are feared and have always
been an endangered species.
Wake up, li'l bruthas! You have royal blood
running through your veins.
You were born to excel despite the depth of your pain.
Hold your head up and step forward to put on your crown.
Faith and self-awareness will never hold you down.
Wake up, li'l bruthas. *Wake up.*

Chapter 14

You Kept Me

After hitting rock bottom it was time for a change. Not knowing where else to turn, my instincts took me back to a place of familiarity, wanting to feel something. Nothing more, nothing less.

Initially, my comfort level led me back to the Catholic Church. It was hard not to hold Mama's death against her killers father. Every time our eyes met all I saw was his son. Some part of me was blaming him.

Father Manny also knew I was struggling and searching for answers. He understood the resolution being sought would not be found there. Father always saw something in me that I couldn't see in myself.

I specifically recall him saying, "If the Catholic Church allowed women to be ordained, you'd be the first. Unfortunately, you've always had a calling on your life that the Catholic Church is not prepared to embrace. You must go and find what God has for you."

Was he telling me to completely leave the church? Yes, that's exactly what he was saying. I didn't leave right at that time. My spirit was still hurting, confused, and dead set on rejecting whatever calling God had for me.

Why did I stay! There was always a constant reminder of Mama's death. Maybe it was a way of taking control. Perhaps to remind the murderers family of what he'd done. I represented a living, breathing replica of my mother and was determined not to let them forget! Still angry and searching for a way to cope.

Very few things helped me deal with the anger except my passion for high-speed sports cars. I was in my early twenties and there was a dangerous sense of freedom from hearing the engine roar. It was nothing for me to jump in my vehicle and race down the highway without a care in the world.

My love for fast cars and loud music led me into a radio shop on Woodward in Detroit. I was excited about getting speakers for the back of my new Mazda.

After walking into the store a man said, "Can I help you?"

Yours truly turned toward the voice and saw Dwight Errington Myer's (a.k.a. Heavy D's) twin except this man's name was Darrell. Heavy D was one of my favorite rap artists. He kept it clean and always gave respect to black women.

It wasn't long before interest was lost when he introduced himself as Darrell and asked for my name. At first, I thought. *Let me play this out for a minute*, that is until he started trying to talk like a playa. It was so obvious he didn't have game.

I decided to give this guy a hard time and simply said, "I don't have a name, but I'm looking for some car speakers. Here's the brand and model number."

For sure that would be the end of any attempts to engage me in conversation. Dray and I were still trying to get over the death of Mama and didn't need anyone new in our lives.

I continued looking around while Darrell checked to see if the speakers were in stock. He finally informed me they weren't, but with a small down payment he could order them. Without thinking, I completed the deposit slip.

When my transaction was finished, I proceeded to walk out the door when Darrell popped the question. "Before you leave, can I get your number?"

I said, "no."

"Well, can I give you mine," he quickly responded.

The only thing that ran through my mind at that moment was, *This guy is not going to give up*. I turned and said, "If giving me your number means getting out of here then yes, by all means, give it to me!"

He wrote it on the back inside cover of a matchbook. Without looking, I tossed it into my purse before giving a sarcastic *goodbye*.

Later that evening, while home watching television, the red light began blinking on my answering machine. That was prior to voicemail. I was engrossed in a lifetime movie and half-heartedly listened to the message. Before the person hung up he said, "You have a lovely day."

After replaying it, the voice on the other end said something about seeing beyond my tough demeanor. My assumption was someone had the wrong number because I hadn't given mine out to anyone.

After that day, a few more messages were left on the recorder. Always ending with the same phrase, "You have a lovely day."

It wasn't until a few weeks later, while switching purses, that I came across the matchbook. Out of pure boredom, I called the number. Darrell answered the phone, and we ended up talking until the wee hours of the morning. It was the first time I recalled laughing that hard since my mother died.

Just as we were about to hang up, he said it! "You have a lovely day."

At that very moment, I realized it was him leaving the messages. Initially, there was laughter but it quickly became anger. How did he get my number.

This man had no way of knowing why I reacted that way. There was something frightening about someone lifting all my information off a deposit slip. My anger didn't last long, and I really enjoyed talking and laughing with Darrell. One night turned into one week, one month, one year.

Once again, here was someone who genuinely seemed to care about my well-being. At some point, I was in a car accident where someone ran into the back of me and totaled my vehicle. Darrell offered his older model car while he either borrowed his mother's or caught the bus to work. He also supported my brother with sending me back to college to complete my bachelor's degree.

I felt so *loved* and thought, *this must be my prince charming*. After we were together for a while, Darrell asked me to marry him a couple of times. I was cautious and declined even though he seemed to truly love me.

Growing up, it was rare to see a successful marriage. In my mind, it didn't exist. Why risk getting into a relationship that was likely to end in an ugly divorce. I predicted we might last two years at the most.

Well that didn't happen. Our relationship kept getting stronger. We started spending more time together and ended up moving in together. Darrell continued helping with school cost and academic achievement. After a while it became obvious that we complimented each other. Everything seemed to be falling in place for our future.

School was going well, and commencement activities were nearing. Employment opportunities seemed plentiful and I was looking forward to obtaining my first career position.

Just before the college graduation ceremony, I applied for and was hired into my first professional job. The position was located about one hour from where I lived in Detroit. I made the commute for a while before transferring to a location that was much closer. This made it easier for me and Darrell to coordinate our work schedules.

We were both hard working individuals and by this time settled into a comfortable lifestyle together. The topic of marriage and children became a more serious discussion as we talked about family dynamics. What would our family structure look like? Neither of us had children and didn't want to have more than we could afford.

Darrell and I also agreed that no matter how our relationship turned out, we would only have children with each other. From that point, it took no time for Darrell to make his marriage proposal again. This time, I accepted his proposal and began making wedding plans.

Me and one of Darrell's sisters, Beth, became very close. She was my little sister and more excited about wedding plans than we were. Beth jumped right into action looking at dates, creating guest lists and solidifying a color scheme.

Liz would make my wedding gown and all the brides maids dresses. Of course, she would be my maid of honor. Sue would provide wedding ideas and help with whatever was needed.

We were full steam ahead and began finalizing things for one year out when the unexpected happened. I was tired all the time and often felt sick. Wait! I know this feeling. It couldn't be! Yes, it was. A pregnancy test confirmed that we were expecting a baby. I was so overjoyed!

This time, I was determined to bring my child into the world. This time, I was having my baby!

It was the most exciting time of our lives We were going to have a little bundle of joy. Things were perfect at home, but work was turning into a nightmare.

My job was located in an area known for lack of diversity and blatant racial discrimination. It was insignificant that I was a top performing employee. An individual that frequently stayed two (2) months or more ahead in work performance.

The building had multiple levels and I was the only person of color housed on the first floor. My work-space was located where everyone could easily observe me. I was strategically isolated from the other black staff who were on the second level of the building. I'm sure this was a tactic designed to keep others from warming me about the company's unfair labor practices.

It didn't matter because I quickly built a number of relationships despite the intentional effort to keep me separated. All the black staff were excited after learning about my pregnancy. They frequently came down to the area where I worked for a brief chat during breaks.

Eventually I began spending a lot of time with a particular colleague. She was deemed to have poor performance by the senior management team.

To provide a visual, the senior management team was defined as three white men. They took pleasure in making sexist, racist jokes, and had no problem with everyone knowing it.

One day, I was called into the director's office where all three men were waiting. My nerves were shot because being summoned by either of the senior managers typically meant trouble. What did they want with me? My case load was two months ahead.

After barely stepping into the office they clearly instructed me to discontinue association with my colleague. I questioned the legality of what was being requested and noted my work performance had never been negatively impacted by interaction with any team members.

It was at that point the three men became angry and provided more specific instructions.

"Tell you what," one of them began, "From now on, don't leave your cubicle without one of us giving you permission."

"You can't do that," I responded. "It's illegal. What if I need to go to the bathroom?"

"You heard what he said," another one touted. "I don't care if you piss on yourself. You need our permission before leaving your cubicle. Even to take a break or go to lunch. You got that?"

"No, I don't got that," I shouted before storming out of the office.

Lunch time was no better. It was horrible! The local police made a habit of following the black employees during lunch or at the end of work hours.

I was so upset. How could they get away with this? I'd heard rumors but it was worse than anyone could imagine. Not knowing what to do, I prayed for a miracle. That's exactly what was received.

One of the white staff overheard the unfair demands and got word to me to do everything that was being asked. At first, I was completely confused by the instructions. She wanted me to call her desk phone to relay a message (e.g., "I am requesting permission to go to the restroom"). She would record it in writing verbatim and provide me with a copy before giving to one of the managers.

This went on for weeks, and my stress level was barely manageable. Eventually, I collected enough documentation and went to both the union and multiple external organizations to file a discrimination claim. My grievance with the union was handled poorly and rendered no resolve.

Thank goodness I had the wherewithal to file an external unfair treatment complaint resulting in all three managers being investigated.

This should have been the happiest time of my life, but it was clouded by severe stress. The situation caused my doctor to take me off work. I was struggling mentally and physically.

About six months into the pregnancy, Darrell and I went for our regular prenatal checkup. The look on the nurse's face immediately caused concern. She left the room and returned with the doctor.

I began crying. Everyone tried to calm me down, but I was unable to hear anything. Darrell had to hold me down so the doctor could put more gel on my stomach. The horrified look on his face said everything.

Overwhelming grief was the only way to describe our emotions! Darrell was taking it really hard and crying too. That was horrific news and we couldn't believe the words coming out of the doctor's mouth.

"I'm so sorry but there is no sign of a heartbeat." We were devastated!

To make things worse, the doctor began explaining how I was too far along to terminate and would need to have induced labor. Now I was angry and hysterical.

"What? You mean I have to actually go into labor and give birth to a dead baby? Are you crazy! I want it out of me *now*!"

All I heard was the doctor telling Darell how it couldn't be done until Monday. Since it was Friday, I would have to go through the entire weekend knowing there was no life inside of me.

I went into denial over the weekend and a deeper depression. No words or actions could bring me out of it. My only thought was this is my punishment for having an abortion. Forgiving myself was out of the question.

Monday finally arrived. As I was being checked into the hospital, it felt like having an out-of-body experience. To top things off, we were put into a room on the same floor as other women giving birth. How cruel! All I could hear was babies crying. It sent me into complete withdrawal. Liz, Sue and Beth were there. They tried to provide comfort, but it was to no avail.

I was so caught up in my own pain I couldn't even think about what Darrell was going through. He was so strong trying to hold it together for me. That all ended when I went into labor and discharged our dead baby. Darrell was right there and saw the whole thing. He knew if they allowed me to see anything, I might go into my own little world and never return.

My fiancé demanded they immediately remove the baby and ran into the bathroom to break down. I could hear him crying. My heart broke for him, but I was in such a depressed state and unable to give comfort.

That was a difficult and painful time in our relationship. I felt like we would never recover, and marriage was not our destiny. However, the experience only brought us closer. We got past the loss of our first child, although he remained in our hearts forever.

When it came time to go back to work, the anxiety was overwhelming. I had not spoken with anyone from the job since being on leave and had no clue what to expect.

Upon return to work, I learned that the investigation of the three managers led to them no longer being employed. I doubt they were terminated and were probably forced to retire. That is a privilege that many of us will never have.

The new manager came to personally greet me and apologized for everything I had to endure. Everyone knew about the discriminatory practices but were afraid to do anything. She asked if there was anything she could do for me.

Without hesitation, I said, "Yes! Get me the heck away from this side of Eight Mile."

She obliged and I ended up being promoted into the area of my choice.

After all that, it seemed there was nothing Darrell and I couldn't conquer. He was truly my friend and a source of strength when I needed it the most.

Ultimately, we were able to continue plans for our wedding. This time there was a need to do things differently. I didn't want any future children born out of wedlock. We immediately began resuming our plans for a garden wedding. There would be a mixture of traditional and African themes. The actual exchange of vows would take place inside the church. I was still a member of the Catholic church, so this was traditional. I didn't know why, but saying our vows inside the church became important to me.

Planning a wedding is like preparing for any other major event. There were many twists and turns. It was both overwhelming and exciting at the same time. Everyone wanted this day to be perfect for me.

Needless to say there was *good* tension in the air as my special day drew near. The ceremony would take place in a beautiful garden at the Fisher Mansion in Detroit. A newly opened banquet hall was also secured at a very reasonable cost.

My aunt Hazel from Chicago agreed to stand in the gap for Mama. Dray would walk me down the aisle as I serenaded Darrell. Every detail had been strategically designed.

Finally, the day we all worked so hard for arrived. Darrell and I went to the church to say our vows. Dray, Liz and Beth were witnesses. Afterwards, the limo drove us ladies to the Fischer Mansion.

The garden was beautiful with lots of natural greenery, flowers, arches, and stairwells. There were even live peacocks. The weather was perfect with lots of sunlight, making our wedding day a memorable occasion.

I truly enjoyed our special day, but have to admit, was glad when it was over. We could now look forward to our new future together.

As time went on, we were both enjoying married life. I didn't think it could get much better until the day of my annual checkup.

My nurse collected routine samples and the doctor conducted his typical exam. Afterwards, I got dressed and went into his office to discuss any results, as usual.

Dr. Lee. looked at me and said, "How are you feeling today?"

"I'm great, thanks for asking," I stated.

He teasingly asked, "How's married life?"

With great pride I said, "I'm loving it."

Dr. Lee. looked at me with a huge smile and asked a strange question. "Are you looking forward to having children?"

With a curious look on my face, I responded "I can't wait."

Well, Dr. Lee. interjected while leaning back in his chair. "It looks like you're on your way. Congratulations!"

I screamed so loud a couple of nurses came running into the room. When they saw me laughing and crying, no words had to be spoken. Tears of joy came streaming down their faces. Everyone knew the horrific situation with my previous pregnancy.

After returning home, I shared the news with Darrell. We were both happy and scared at the same time, but our excitement overcame any fears. The one thing I knew for sure was that I was going to do everything in my power to bring our child safely into this world.

As you can see, I was no angel, but somehow there were angels all around, assigned specifically to me. I knew in my heart God had his hands on me. It wouldn't be until much later that I'd come to realize the very entity I was running away from would be the one to help rescue me from myself.

You may be wondering, "How do you know God had his hands on you?" It's simple! There were just so many traumatic and dangerous situations that others had become fatal victims to. For some reason, I kept being spared.

For instance, Darrell and I had a combined income, sufficient enough to adequately support a family of four. We purchased a beautiful bungalow on the eastside of Detroit. The upstairs was knotty pine. I claimed this as my getaway area. The basement was completely finished, and quite naturally, Darrell claimed it as his *man cave.*

We were living in our home for about one week when there was a knock at the side door. Darrell went to check, and it was someone who said he was our neighbor. I slowly walked in their direction to hear what was going on. The man began asking if we knew there was a tree laying on the front of our home. I looked at Darrell with that he-don't-know-us-to-be-joking-like-that kind of look.

Our neighbor must have picked up on my facial expression. He immediately asked us to go look out the front door but cautioned not to open it. Sure enough, we could see nothing but branches.

We hurriedly put on some clothes, went out the side door, walked to the front of the house and right into a crowd of folks who heard the tree uprooting. It ripped out a large portion of the street and sidewalk; yet we were in the back of the house and didn't hear a thing.

There was an older couple that lived across the street and witnessed everything. They described it as if the tree was slowly placed on the house like *someone* or *something* gently laid it down.

It was the largest tree on the block with rotted roots, so it should have smashed through the home. We likely would not have survived the crash or would have been seriously injured.

When I tell you there was not a single window broken or any damage to the roof, I mean nothing. The only loss was to the basement foundation because the roots of the tree were so big, they pulled the wall out.

Everyone standing around kept telling us how lucky we were. I knew it was more than luck. Something supernatural occurred on that day. I started recalling all the harmful situations God kept me from. This prompted a sudden and pressing desire to have a different mindset.

You Kept Me

I wanted to walk down a path full of joy and laughter; yet the road paved for me had many twists, turns, and sorrows. When thoughts insisted on pulling me back into yesterday, you kept pushing me toward tomorrow. You kept me when my actions put me in harm's way. You kept me when my spirit wandered down dark and dreary roads. You kept me when I was alone and pain was trying to overtake me. You whispered and called me by my name.

You kept me!

Chapter 15

Miracles

Awaiting Shay's Arrival

As events of the past few months began to evaporate, we started focusing on our pregnancy. It was apparent that Darrell was anxious. He also knew I was scared until we reached the six-month mark. There was still a very strong heartbeat. The baby was doing flips, which thrilled me whenever my stomach did water waves. That was how I kept my sanity.

If *she* didn't move within so many hours, I would wake her up by shaking my stomach or eating a little sugar. It always worked. Then something strange began to happen. My balance was completely off, resulting in accidental collapses for no reason. One bad fall caused a serious fracture to my right hip. Doctor Lee immediately took me off work as a high-risk pregnancy with restricted movement.

I was not allowed to drive or leave the house unless someone was with me. If it required walking, the person (mostly my husband) had to grip my arm very firmly to prevent an accidental fall. My mattress was put on the floor so I could crawl to the bathroom. I had to shower with assistance. Ironically, none of this bothered me.

My only concern was giving birth to a healthy baby girl. Excitement literally kept a sincere smile on my face even when emotions tried to get the best of me. Thank goodness for Beth, Sue and Liz.

Sue and Liz kept me grounded with soothing and encouraging words. I was consumed with not being able to protect my child. Neither of them knew exactly why at the time.

Beth practically lived with us and helped plan the baby shower which stimulated lots of excitement.

The enthusiasm must have been contagious because we had the type of event I'd never been to before. It was coed! Darrell and his best friend wanted to be there. It was so much fun. I never thought men would enjoy actively participating in a baby shower.

After it was over we were able to refocus. I felt a strong desire to begin training one of my dogs. The purpose was to protect my baby when she arrived into this world.

Her name would be Scha'Kerra, like her older cousin, and we'd call her Shay for short.

I completely trusted my dogs, Precious and Ms. Bear. Strange, right? I didn't know why, I just knew one of them had to be trained.

Ms. Bear was older and having some health challenges, so I began training Precious, my Chow Chow. Everyone kept telling me that Chow Chows weren't good with children, and I would have to get rid of her. My spirit was telling me differently.

Darrell purchased a baby doll, blanket, and powder. After spreading the cover on the floor, I laid the doll on it and sprinkled a very small amount of powder. Precious was taught to lay and protect without getting on the blanket. She was only allowed to touch the edges.

Precious got really good with commands and understood the word *protect*. I'll tell you more about what happened momentarily.

The time of going into labor was growing near. I began having what I thought to be contractions, but they were known as Braxton-Hicks. These are extreme intermittent cramps women have during pregnancy. In short, false labor.

There came a time when I had this sudden burst of energy and went into a cleaning frenzy. Darrell helped me move from one area of the house to another. I cleaned the stove, refrigerator, behind appliances, everything. It took the whole day because I had to sit while cleaning.

Then it happened! My water broke and the real contractions started. We already had a bag packed, so it was just a matter of Darrell getting me to the hospital.

Once we arrived, I was taken straight into a beautiful labor and delivery birthing room. The contractions started getting stronger, and my blood pressure spiked. My feet and body were severally swollen due to pregnancy-induced toxemia.

The labor was really difficult because I was made to lay on my right side and couldn't get up and move around like other women. There was fear of me falling. I laid on my right side as long as I could before begging to go to the bathroom. They wanted me to use a pan, but my mind just wouldn't let *it* happen.

Eventually, the nurse allowed Darrell to help me into the bathroom. I locked the door, refusing to let anyone in. I just needed to stand up and move around.

The nurse said the magic words, "You could injure the baby."

Without thought, I unlocked the door, came out of the bathroom, and crawled back into bed.

It didn't take much longer before I was told, "You're at ten. The baby's coming, push."

I pushed with all my might, and she just popped out. Shay was a beautiful little bundle of joy and was the spitting image of her father. It was like "Daddy's baby, Momma's maybe." I couldn't see me anywhere, but it didn't matter...*we did it!*

Shay was handed to me momentarily before one of the attending nurses picked my baby up. She took Shay out of the room, and started showing her to everyone. Dray was waiting out by the nurses station and hurriedly came into the room. The look on my face immediately signaled to my husband and brother that the nurse was about to be in big trouble.

I tried to get out the bed, but my family wouldn't let me. I believe it was either Darrell or my brother who advised her to bring my baby back before all hell broke loose.

She kept apologizing and trying to explain. I wasn't trying to hear any of that. "You're a nurse and should know better," I yelled. All I could think about is, *What if you accidentally dropped her?* Nothing would have kept me from rising up out of that bed.

I kept my baby in the room with me during the entire hospital stay, carefully watching over her. Unexpectedly, a gripping fear came over me, and I couldn't pick Shay up. How was I going to protect her from all the sick people in the world? Who was going to help me and Darrell raise her? Who would be our village? Everyone we trusted was still in the workforce. How could I go back to work outside the home and trust anyone else with her?

All of these questions were sweeping through my mind and numbed me. Shay was screaming, but my body was frozen. A nurse came running in the room to see why she was crying so loudly. I burst into tears and explained that I couldn't pick her up. I was afraid about not being able to protect her.

The nurse was so empathetic. She did a great job explaining how it was normal to be a little fearful, but that I would make a great mom. It was apparent I wanted the best for my child.

What she didn't know was how warped my mind had become from past experiences. Working in a field that provided first-hand knowledge about childhood abuse shaped my views. I knew the possibilities. A large percentage of child sexual abuse occurred by people closest to the family. It wasn't strangers that frightened me. Finding another alternative for income was my only option.

I became familiar with some of the leave policies and took full advantage. This allowed me to stay off work a significant amount of time. During this period I opened an in-home licensed childcare service. It was a great experience. Beth helped on a regular basis when she was not working. Parents loved having their children there.

When my approved leave was nearing its end, customers were notified so they would have enough time to locate another program. Many of them cried because we provided more than just child-care. Our team focused on the whole family and offered love to them and their children.

I was a nervous wreck as the expiration of my leave drew near. Darrell worked evenings so we didn't have to worry about daycare. Nonetheless, he wasn't me. Darell was inexperienced, and my baby was a little girl! He wasn't going to take all the precautions I would. Admittedly I was overly protective, paranoid, and suspicious of everyone. No one was excluded, not family or friends.

My background provided me with more insight than the average person. It mentally tormented me when it came to the safety of my own child.

Sue, who was a tremendous friend and sister, initially didn't understand all the concern. She quickly came to realize that it was my own traumatic experiences and knowledge of child molestation that had me so frazzled with fear. Sue was a great support. She remained very patient until I became comfortable enough to allow Shay out of my sight. Her name was Auntie Sue from Shay's date of birth until now.

When it came time for return to work, we mapped out a plan. I didn't live far from my job. Most days, I'd use my lunch break to run home and check on Shay. Every Friday was a sigh of relief.

The weekends were filled with joy just watching her play and grow. My two dogs were my children prior to having Shay. Ms. Bear took on the role of guarding Precious, so as I previously mentioned, I taught Precious to be Shay's protector by defending the entire area around the baby doll.

It was quite hilarious when Shay took the place of the doll, which didn't move or cry. Precious didn't know what to make of this breathing, moving, and crying little person. Her initial reaction was to run out of the room. She would return and peek around the corner to see what in the world happened to the other *thing* that didn't move or make noise!

I was very cautious and observant, only allowing baby steps with Precious. After a few weeks, she stopped laying at the entrance of the room. Slowly making her way close to wherever I was sitting with the baby. Once I could clearly see that my dog had become more relaxed, I would sit on the floor with Shay. Precious would lay outside the perimeter of the blanket as she was trained.

She caught on really quickly and even began to respond to the different sounds. If Shay cried, Precious was up and alert, assuring I was responsive. If Shay babbled, Precious wagged her tail in excitement. It became more evident as Shay got older that Precious had fully taken ownership of her role as protector.

I recall sitting on the living room sofa, watching television, while our beautiful little girl was in her Pack-n-Play. Precious laid as close to the Pack-n-Play as possible. Shay suddenly reached up with both arms as if someone were reaching to pick her up. Her bodyguard began barking, growling, and snapping at something.

My baby was still reaching and laughing. Precious abruptly stopped barking and sat at attention as if I'd given the command, but I didn't.

From that very moment, I was convinced that an angel had been assigned to protect my baby, just like Precious.

This was not the only incident of its kind. It seemed Shay had a similar gift as me. She could see things. I could already tell she was going to be a take-charge type of individual.

As time went on, Shay was becoming more active. She began paying attention to everything and was really inquisitive. That's what toddlers do.

I was at work one day and Darrell was home with our daughter. He apparently put her down for a nap. After she fell asleep, he decided to take a nap as well. At some point, Shay woke up and decided to take Precious for a walk. She put on her raincoat, rain boots, put the leash on the dog and proceeded to exit the house.

Shay made it to the main street, which was extremely busy with speeding cars. A woman noticed her trying to cross the street. Precious was continuously circling to prevent her from crossing. The woman tried to get close, but the dog would not allow her.

Within minutes, Darrell came flying around the corner in a panic. He witnessed our dog doing the job she was trained to do. My husband jumped out the car, barely acknowledging the woman. He began hugging Shay and Precious before quickly putting them in his car and driving off.

I eventually found out the whole ordeal a few days after it happened. Darrell was smart enough not to tell me right away. Once he did share, I was furious. It took a minute for me to become more grateful than angry. I'm amazed it wasn't the end of my marriage. According to Darrell, he was in a deep sleep when something (felt like someone) shook the bed really hard. For a reason unknown to him, he jumped up in a panic and immediately went to check on Shay. She was not there. Almost out of instinct, he ran to the front door. It was locked. When he got to the side door, fear almost overcame him. The side door was standing wide open, and Precious was nowhere to be found.

After this incident, we had an alarm system installed with chimes. I also made the decision to put Shay in daycare.

This was such a frightening process. I knew all too well that some facilities employed unqualified individuals to care for children. Fortunately, my cousin Niecy worked at a nice childcare center. It just so happened that Shay would be placed in her class. I felt confident she would be well taken care of and would receive lots of love. If Niecy didn't go to work, Shay didn't go to daycare. Flat out!

Awaiting Cierra's Arrival

Things seemed to be working well, so Darrell and I began talking about having another child. He had a big family and felt it wasn't right for Shay to grow up without siblings.

I agreed and we began planning for our next child. By this time, Our daughter had just turned three (3). My aunt Mary, who had terminal cancer, moved in with us under hospice care. She loved Shay and enjoyed having her around. It seemed our child was the only one that could get auntie to eat, bathe, or do anything.

Aunt Mary's pleasant disposition drastically changed as her illness began taking control of her body. I knew she was in a lot of pain and understood the change. However, she was like putty in Shay's hands. Auntie always had a heart for children and practically raised my little cousin Tierra.

On one occasion, I was trying to lift my aunt to change her. Out of nowhere, she gained strength to fight and refused to let me raise her. By this time, it had become difficult for Aunt Mary to speak so I couldn't understand why Auntie was fighting. She seemed stronger and more powerful than ever.

She forced the words out, "You're going to hurt the baby."

I said, "Auntie, Shay is right here. She's okay."

Aunt Mary looked at me and shook her head no. What happened next was nothing short of amazing. Auntie pointed at my stomach. I immediately understood and stopped everything. Darrell lifted my aunt and helped me change the bed. Right away, she stopped fighting.

After we got auntie settled, I ran out the house to get a pregnancy test. Sure enough, the test showed a positive result. This was also confirmed after my visit to the doctor's office.

I couldn't wait to tell Aunt Mary. I went straight to her room and began talking fifty miles per minute with excitement. She smiled and nodded her head in agreement.

A joy came over her that only happened when she was with Shay. Shortly after, auntie died. Although she was very sick, no one was prepared for her death. Not emotionally or financially. Auntie didn't have an insurance policy, and I had little money saved. What were we going to do?

About a week later, I was at Aunt Mary's apartment, cleaning up. Shay (still three years old) went into Auntie's bedroom and began having a full-blown conversation with someone. We were the only ones in the apartment, so I knew what was happening. I slowly approached the bedroom door and asked Shay who she was talking to.

"I'm talking to Aunt Mary," Shay replied. "She told me to tell you about the money."

Surprised, I said, "What money?"

"In the freezer!" Shay innocently said.

I went straight to the refrigerator, opened the freezer door, and looked everywhere but couldn't find anything. Finally, I thought, *This is absurd. Why would she put money in the freezer?*

Shay kept saying, "Mommy, Auntie said look in the freezer."

I played along and said, "Mommy did look, baby. There's nothing there."

Shay was walking toward the kitchen as if she was holding someone's hand and kept insisting, "Mommy look in the freezer."

I picked her up so she could see inside. After putting her back down, she ran to the small freezer chest and said, "Not that freezer, Mommy, this one! Auntie said it's not inside the freezer, it's on the side of it."

Again, I looked all around the freezer and didn't see anything until I noticed what looked like a small door at the bottom. I slid the door back and located a money bag. There was a total of $2,500 in the bag. I hugged and kissed Shay and told her to tell Aunt Mary thank you. She did just that and went back into the bedroom to finish her conversation with Auntie while I continued to clean up.

When it was time to go, I asked Shay what she talked to Auntie about. Apparently, Aunt Mary told her she was having a little sister and they were going to be really close. Shay insisted she was going to be *a good big sister*. I agreed and said, "Yes, you will."

Do I believe Shay was talking to Aunt Mary? No. But I do believe she had a supernatural occurrence. An event with someone she could identify with in order not to frighten her. The experience was real. There was no way a small child could have known the details of what was revealed that day.

It was this encounter that set my baby on a mission as a three-year old. There was something about being a good big sister that gave her a sense of pride. We also had an unforeseen situation that would provide Shay with a big sister figure of her own.

Who knew, at the very time we were set on having a second child, we'd gain a third. I unexpectedly found myself unprepared to help raise an adolescent!

Ironically, my niece Scha'kerra (Ke-Ke), came to live with my brother and I from Guam. She was twelve at the time me and Dray became her co-guardians. We hadn't seen her since she was an infant before Tony died.

The transition would be difficult because she didn't really know us. I can only imagine what that must have felt like for her. Being in a strange place with people who call themselves your family, but you have no memory of them.

Thankfully, she really took a liking to Shay. Ke-Ke almost immediately took on a big sister role. I think it gave her a feeling of belonging.

I was overjoyed to have Ke-Ke back with us, but there was a lack of trust on all our parts. Just as she didn't know anything about us, we didn't know a lot about her background or home environment. It wasn't easy building a trusting relationship, but we loved her and were committed to trying.

The one thing that ultimately became apparent, was Ke-Ke genuinely loved Shay. She was a big help keeping her little cousin occupied and excited about the expected arrival of her new cousin. Shay's enthusiasm and Ke-Ke's arrival helped me to stay energetic.

This time, my pregnancy was not as difficult. I was much more active, although still a high-risk pregnancy. I wasn't falling like before, but I couldn't walk straight. There was usually someone walking on both sides of me, if walking any distance. This was to help me walk without veering to the left or right.

The excitement and fear about this pregnancy was just as amazing/scary as it was when we got pregnant with Shay. Initially there was the lingering thought of "what if something goes wrong?" Those thoughts didn't last long. The baby was very active and had no problems making her existence known.

My stomach was like an ocean of huge waves during the day and a calm sea at night. This gave me some indication of what her sleep pattern would be. She was not interested in eating different types of food as indicated by the sickness experienced throughout my pregnancy. However, I recall one dish she seemed to enjoy.

There was a restaurant down the street from where I worked. They would prepare a special dish of rice with some type of spicy chicken and seafood sauce on it. This was my daily nutrient while at work and home. Every now and then, I'd throw in something different. Always risking not being able to hold it down. It's funny, Shay wanted to help every step of the way. Even when I got sick.

She'd rub my stomach and talk to "her baby" as if Cierra (aka CJ) was standing right in front of us. Shay always contended that this was going to be her baby.

I remember her saying, "Mommy, I'm going to help feed her, change her diaper, and be the best big sister."

The sisterly relationship started way before birth. Little sister responded every time she heard Shay's voice or felt her touch. The night I went into labor was no different. Cierra seemed to respond to the excitement in her big sister's voice.

The time finally arrived. My water broke and Darrell prepared us for the hospital trip. We chose to have a birthing room experience where all family members could be present up until the time of delivery. I made sure Ke-Ke and another niece, Kassaundra, stayed during the delivery. This was just in case they were thinking about becoming sexually active any time soon.

They both had lots of questions and wanted to know everything. What was intended to be a lesson on tough love, turned out to be a lesson of love from them to me. They waited patiently for Cierra's moment of arrival.

CJ was stubborn. I was in labor for two days. She didn't want to experience this world just yet. I was adamant about not taking any medications, but the pain got too intense. Ultimately, I caved and allowed the doctors to give me an epidural. Within minutes, CJ began spinning down the birth canal.

Something about the trip must have scarred her because the doctor began yelling, "She's going back up."

Is that even possible! I didn't know a baby could spin back up the birth canal. I heard the doctor say, "We're going to have to guide her out."

He grabbed this tool that made me scream *no*! "I'll push her out. Don't use those things on my baby."

Darrell and a nurse had to literally hold my legs up so I could push because the epidural caused temporary paralysis.

At last, CJ made her arrival with a loud cry that was music to all our ears. She was fighting mad with fist balled and screaming to the top of her lungs. What a beautiful sight.

Once again, my mind started wandering to the question of *How am I going to protect my children?* Seeing Shay helped shift my thoughts.

On day two in the hospital, Shay was eager to hold *her baby*. She climbed into a chair, as if knowing what to do, and reached out both arms. Of course, I sat with her as we held baby girl together. Shay reiterated how she was going to be the best big sister ever. I looked at her with so much love, knowing she meant every word.

It came time for us to take CJ home from the hospital. Darrell and I set up a beautiful nursery, which included a full-size bed for me. I had *mommy ears* and could hear every sound (breathing, whimpering, moving). This wasn't unusual as I became a really light sleeper when Shay was born. It seemed like I literally slept with one eye open.

Cierra didn't like sleeping by herself much and made sure everyone knew it. I learned to wrap her tightly in a swaddle for comfort. There was something about not being close to mommy that didn't sit well with her. Our little bundle of joy would sleep soundly in her crib for about thirty (30)-minute spurts before waking up and demanding to be held. Yes, she was a lap baby!

Once baby sister was a few months old, Shay began asking about changing diapers and assisting with feeding. I was somewhat shocked. Even though Shay talked about helping before her sister was born, it was unusual for a three-year old.

Most kids run away from the smell of a dirty diaper, so I compromised. CJ was still too little for her big sister to handle. Shay was excited after being put in charge of placing the feeding pillow under my arm when it was time to nurse. She also got a kick out of helping me pump milk into bottles.

When Cierra's head became stable, Shay was allowed to hold her with supervision. It's also important to note that Precious jumped right into action. She understood her role, but never strayed too far from her best friend, Shay.

I took another extended leave from work and reopened my in-home daycare facility. Family life was wonderful! Darrell was a hard worker and provider and supported me being a work-at-home mother for a year.

I give credit to parents who make that choice. It is one of the hardest jobs I've ever had. It was also one of the most rewarding.

Cierra was a very happy yet observant baby. She had a keen sense of people and would only interact with those invited into her world. From birth, CJ demonstrated the gift to discern spirits. There were those she absolutely refused to engage with, others she slowly warmed up to, and some she immediately bonded with. This was few and far between, as witnessed at her baby dedication.

Things were going great until it was time for me to return to work. My situation was the same as with Shay. Petrified about who to leave my child with. Niecy was no longer working at the daycare center where Shay attended. Now I was ready to quit my job.

I'm unsure how it happened, but at the right moment, one of my neighbors and I were having a conversation. She had very well-mannered children. They were homeschooled due to similar concerns. It was a big surprise when I found out her home was licensed to provide child-care services.

She seemed to love children and I always admired the patience shown with her kids and others on the block. Talk about a ram in the bush!

After completing a thorough background search, I enrolled Cierra in my neighbor's daycare. This made it easy for me and Darrell to drop by for random check-ins. CJ remained in the program until we moved back into my family home.

Yes, this was the same home where I previously felt so empty and refused to live there after Mama died. Now I wanted nothing more but to feel her presence in that house. We moved in during the summer months. This gave us an opportunity to get settled before school started. CJ was going to be starting pre-school and Shay second grade.

Both of my children were enrolled into a private school where they received a wonderful education. This didn't just happen because they were sent to a good school. I was a very involved parent, interested in the success of my children.

I started a coed basketball team to stay involved, which the children and parents seemed to enjoy. The school was small, and many of the parents were very close. To supplement tuition costs, I negotiated with the school's president to write a grant for a new technology lab. Funds were successfully obtained, and the school established a beautiful state of the art lab.

Family life was great! My children were healthy and happy. Finances were plentiful and I started embracing whatever life had to offer.

Mommy, I Love You

"Mommy?"
"Yes, dear."
"Do I have to go to school today?"
"Are you sick?"
"No."
"Is there something wrong at school?"
"No."
"Then why don't you want to go to school?"
"Because I'm still sleepy."
"Oh! In that case, yes, you do have to go to school."
"But why?"
"Because education is the road to your independence."

"Mommy?"
"Yes, sweetheart."
"Do I have to go to bed?"
"Yes."
"But why? I'm not sleepy."
"Because you need your sleep so that you can grow big and strong."

"Mommy?"
"Yes, honey."
"Do I have to go to my room? I won't do it again."
"Yes, you do, baby."

"But why? I didn't color the whole wall."
"Because you have to learn that the decisions
you make have consequences."

"Mommy?"
"Yes, darling."
"Can I have some candy?"
"No, not right now."
"Why? I didn't put them in glitter this time."
"Because I'm your mother and I said no."

"Mommy?"
"Yes, sugar."
"What is a miracle?"
"A work of God, like you and your sister."

"Mommy?"
"*What!*"
"…I love you."

Chapter 16

I'm Still Here

It was after our move home that God placed yet another strong woman in my life—Rhonda. She helped to open my mind, seize the moment, and take advantage of life's traveling opportunities. It was because of her that I got on an airplane to travel to the Million Woman March in Pennsylvania.

It was hilarious! We arrived at Metro Airport so early that we saw the pilots and attendants preparing to board the flight.

Leaning towards Rhonda, I said, "I need to ask them some questions."

She immediately said, "Girl, don't embarrass me."

"I won't," was my reply.

Politely walking up to the pilots, I began explaining my fear of flying and asked if they would mind answering a few questions. The pilots and flight attendants all welcomed the questions. "Okay, here goes...

Do you believe you've had enough rest to properly fly this aircraft? Have you had any legal or illegal substances that would impair your ability to fly this aircraft? How many years of experience do you have flying? During your years of experience, have you ever faced a situation that warranted an emergency landing?"

The questions were shot out so fast, it caused them to laugh hysterically. Rhonda was completely embarrassed. Once they gained their composure, each of them took turns answering the questions and ended up changing our seats to first class.

The atttendants were more than attentive, assuring we were comfortable and that my anxiety wasn't too high. There was nothing they could really do about my fear, but the customer service was outstanding!

I must explain that my fear was not without good cause. Dray was out of town in August 1987 and scheduled to return home on Northwest Flight 255. He was running late and missed his plane. Later that evening, Northwest Flight 255 crashed at Metro Airport, killing about 156 people. There was only one survivor, a little four (4)-year old girl named Cecelia.

This was one (1) year to the month Mama was killed. I was frantic trying to get ahold of Dray, but he was not answering his phone. Just as I was giving into the thought that my brother was dead, the phone rang. It was Dray. He had no idea the plane he missed had crashed and killed all but one passenger.

It was devastating knowing so many families would have to face something so horrific. It made me cry like a baby. I knew all too well the pain of sudden and tragic loss.

God knew I would not mentally survive another tragedy. Thank you, Lord, for sparing my brother. Dray made it back home. Since that day he was always required to call each time he arrived or departed a destination.

Let's get back to family life. It seemed everything was too good to be true. Together, my husband and I had more than enough income. We traveled multiple times per year, and our children were happy and healthy.

It was beneficial having a great boss, Deb. She became my mentor, and friend. Deb eventually recommended me to become the grant coordinator for our county. I was sent out of state to a one-week grant writing workshop and ended up securing funds for two large initiatives. By this time, Shay was about eight and Cierra about four.

We seemed very comfortable with our lifestyle until work-family life became problematic. The job was becoming increasingly demanding and taking more time away from my family. Once the internal struggle between my personal life and job began, it didn't take long for me to make a decision. I first spoke with Darrell about starting my own company. We were both a little nervous about me quitting my job, but he supported it nonetheless.

I went to my director and said, "There's something I'd like to try. Can we talk as though I were your daughter, not your employee?"

Mr. Rully sat straight up in his chair and said, "I would be honored."

Taking a deep breath I said, "I'd like to start my own business doing training and grant writing. I've drafted a business plan and was thinking about taking some time off work to see if I could be successful. What are your thoughts, or how would you advise me if I were your daughter?"

Mr. Rully looked at me thoughtfully and said, "If you were my daughter, I'd tell you there is no choice. You'll never know what you can be successful at unless you try. If you submit a request, I'll approve it and hold your position for one (1) year."

Unbelievable! Not only was he supporting the risk I was about to take, he was also giving me a safety net just in case it didn't work out. There was an enormous amount of faith that flooded my spirit. Immediately the plan was put into motion, and I proceeded to prepare for my business venture.

After setting up shop, out of nowhere, I got a call from an old friend asking if I was in the position to receive grant dollars.

"What! Are you asking if I can provide a service and get paid for doing it? Absolutely!" I responded.

I contracted with a local government agency and became one of their best resources for working with low-income individuals. My company provided job readiness, entrepreneurship, and technology classes. Not just providing the training but also having real outcomes. We assisted students with developing business plans and securing start-up funds for small businesses, obtaining employment, and more.

It didn't stop there. I was selected by the US Department of Justice to oversee a crime reduction program in the city of Detroit.

Our household didn't miss a beat. I stayed involved with my children's school, prepared meals, and took care of my family. My children were always with me and even got a kick out of learning to answer the phone and filing documents.

They looked forward to getting out of school, doing homework, having dinner, and hanging out with Mommy to see what else they would learn. Shay and CJ were definitely children of the community.

If I showed up somewhere without them, the inquisition would start. "Where are they?" "Why aren't they with you?" "Do you need to go get them?" "Don't come back next time without them."

People were always feeding and welcoming us into their homes, especially Marjorie Henry. Thanks, Ms. Henry. I can't think of any better experience than the love we all felt being a part of the community.

Little did I know my children were watching me and their father closely. It would provide them with a great foundation for strong work ethics. Daddy was working hard in property management, and Mommy was an entrepreneur. CJ decided at a very young age she would be the next business owner.

We were like the family on the Cosby Show to outsiders looking in. Even I thought my family had it all together. Boy was that mindset wrong. We started having our fair share of issues, particularly marital ones.

Arguments began about small things at first, then grew in intensity about everything. Money, trust, women, and more. Despite the troubles between me and my husband, being a single parent was not a part of my plans.

Knowing what needed to be done, I set out to find a new church home. One that would dive deeper into Biblical principles and have a strong focus on marriage. There was an attack on our family. I was desperate and needed a church that would help guide us.

Finding the right place of worship was a difficult experience. It should not have been, with more than five thousand in my community. I started in a Pentecostal church, where my gift of speaking things into existence became stronger. It frightened both me and a church member I became really close with.

One night, we were driving together to Bible study when I said, "The pipes just burst in the church."

She looked at me and asked "Why would you say such a thing?"

Honestly, I didn't know what made me speak those words; I just knew it was true. We pulled up to the church, where her husband was waiting for us. He ran up to the minivan we were in and told his wife that the pipes had just burst.

She looked terrified. My buddy jumped out the car, slammed the passenger side door shut and held it there. Her husband was completely baffled until she explained what happened.

He laughed and said, "You act like you've just seen a ghost or something. You do believe in spiritual gifts, don't you?"

I was still a babe in understanding gifts of the Spirit. What I did grasp, was my ability to know things. Apparently, the pastor recognized this as well. He would have me exhort just before preaching. Each time, God provided a preview to his sermon. He and his wife would get so excited.

It was my first time realizing my abilities were a gift, not a curse. I enjoyed the church. It's where my calling to preach the Gospel was more intensely stirred, but not enough to submit.

Unfortunately, my husband was not interested in attending the church. Even so, we kept going because my children were developing loving relationships and I was learning.

We were at the church for a season, but it was not the place where I would be formally trained and mentored. There was a calling on my life that was becoming harder to reject. After a short time the search for another church began.

My family ended up at our first nondenominational church. It was great initially. Especially when Darrell came for a visit and surprisingly joined. We all seemed to enjoy the teachings. I even became a part of the praise team, which I loved. The kids met new friends and Darrell was interacting with strong men of God. Things seemed to be turning around.

Unfortunately, that would prove to be short lived. Trouble was still boiling over in our marriage. Communication was almost non-existent. We lived as roommates, simply co-existing. I couldn't do that to my children. Shay and CJ were no longer witnessing love between their parents.

My daughters were living in a home that lacked the example of parenthood we agreed to provide. Challenges with finances became an issue as we found ourselves in a single income situation. This seemed to weigh heavily on my husband. He was no longer able to provide the same level of support as previously.

Darrell got hurt at work, ended up losing his job, and everything went completely downhill from there. We tried spiritual counseling, professional counseling, talking, arguing, everything! Nothing seemed right anymore. At first, we would only have differences when the children weren't around, then it got progressively worse.

In my mind the only thing that would keep me in a relationship with him was a tragedy. Life and death are in the power of the tongue. A few days later, his grandparents, whom I was very close with, were killed in an auto accident.

Did I cause the accident? No. Would it have happened regardless of whether the those words were spoken or not? Maybe! It didn't stop me from feeling like it was my fault. It caused me to stay in a painful and unstable situation for just a while longer.

I could say it was for the sake of my children, but the truth is, there was a fear of becoming a single parent. What I learned on that day was the tongue truly is sharper than a two-edged sword. I've tried hard to never speak out of anger like that again, and always try to think before responding.

The eighteen-year relationship with my husband came to an end. He left the sanctity of our marriage much sooner than the physical separation came about.

Leaving this partnership was a little different. Darrell was the father of my children. He was also a good friend before becoming my husband. Both came to an end along with our membership at church. It was too difficult worshipping in a place where we'd both established great relationships.

I was living a new reality. There was no time to focus on myself. My two children needed me to be strong and healthy now more than ever. I had no visible signs of sadness, depression, withdrawal, grief, or loss. I just simply functioned and did what had to be done.

My children, particularly Shay, were devastated. Behaviors that weren't there before started surfacing, and it was clear they were angry.

Shay was a daddy's girl and didn't understand why she could no longer live with her father. She did not display any disrespect, it just wasn't something tolerated in our family, but there was a difference. CJ was always very quiet. I couldn't really tell what she was feeling or thinking until her anger surfaced at school. It took a very long time to repair the damage that had been caused. She became angrier at her father and refused to talk to him for years.

I had very little support, financially or otherwise, and was left to be mother and father in many ways. There were feelings of resentment and anger, but the safety and well-being of my children was priority. I neglected my own mental health needs. That was a mistake.

If not for great friends and love for my children, I would've completely collapsed. My growing faith was also sustaining me. However, there was still one thing missing. Another church home.

Instead of running away from God when the storms came, I started running full speed toward Him. I fasted and prayed regularly for God to help me find another church home. One where I could increase my growth even if for a season.

He always answers. We landed at a Baptist church, which traditionally didn't license women ministers. Why I was compelled to become a member of this church was beyond me, but God knew.

After a period of time, He touched the pastor's heart because I was the second female he licensed as an evangelist. Here is also where God sent me a second mother, Arbutus Garwood. She adopted us into her family and claimed me as her own. Momma Garwood coined a nickname that she and my sisters lovingly call me today—Princess.

I stayed at the church for a short while after becoming licensed. Serving faithfully in the choir, on the worship team, and preaching the Word of God. I studied regularly and was like a sponge soaking up all the information. God gave me a unique way to break down the message so that it was understandable to even children.

Imagine that! Me preaching and teaching the Word of God. A serious sinner saved by grace. I had a burning desire to read, study, and help others. Once again, people began revealing hidden secrets they'd never shared before.

My purpose came flooding back to the surface as young women began sharing abuse suffered in childhood. Horrific accounts of interfamilial molestation.

Like me, the shame they felt affected many decisions as a result of their trauma. It guided them into bad relationships and poor choices. This resulted in a cycle of rejection, depression, and anger. I understood all too well the confusion and bad decisions.

Active listening strengthened my gift to look within people to hear and see what they weren't saying. The festering wounds that kept being reopened had to be closed before it destroyed them. Before it destroyed me.

There was a readiness to let go of the anger that was eating me up inside. I prayed to be delivered from it, and once again God answered my prayers. He had already Released me. It was up to me to forgive myself and all those who hurt me.

At first, I resisted the thought of forgiving men who violated my innocence. It was simply beyond my understanding. The greater challenge would be to forgive the man who murdered my mother, Tiree. It wasn't until later that I came to understand forgiveness was more for me than it was for them.

No sooner than the decision was made to try this forgiveness thing, I was tried. The victims' advocate program notified me that Tiree was going before the parole board. He had terminal cancer, and they were seriously considering releasing him but wanted my input. After much thought and internal turmoil, I realized God was testing me. My spirit became driven to somehow witness to the one person that brought me the most harm.

"God, please place the words in my mouth and soften my heart so your will can be done." I prayed.

After picking up the phone I called the number on the letter. A woman answered, identifying herself as Ms. Beesy.

As I begin identifying myself, she interrupted and gently said, "I know exactly who you are. I never thought you'd call."

My stomach became twisted in knots as I began asking questions about Tiree's condition and parole possibility. Ms. Beesy responded to each question, being careful not to breach confidentiality, which was understood.

After about fifteen minutes, Ms. Beesy was asked "Are you a Christian?"

Her response was "yes."

I then asked, "How strong is your faith?"

Her response was, "It's not my faith that's in question, but yours."

The question was then presented to me. "How strong is your faith? Do you have unquestionable faith or is it conditional?"

The words *unquestionable* or *conditional* remain with me until this day. Ms. Beesy was obviously a strong believer. What I said next caused her to cry.

"Ms. Beesy," I said, "Can you get a message to Tiree for me from God? Let him know he's forgiven for killing my mom, but that's not really important. What's more imperative is that he admits his faults to God and ask Him for forgiveness before he leaves this life. Will you do that for me?"

With sobbing and what sounded like tears of joy, Ms. Beesy gave a resounding *yes!* "Yes, I will!"

I thanked Ms. Beesy. Before hanging up, I told her that God is about to do something extraordinary.

Miraculous was the word! A couple weeks after my conversation with Ms. Beesy, a letter came in the mail that was forwarded on behalf of Tiree. It was difficult to open it right away, but when I did, it read:

> What kind of person would forgive some-
> one for murdering their mother? All this time, I
> haven't been able to admit I took the life of some-

one who was nothing but good to me and my family. I was so strung out on drugs and didn't care about nobody but myself and how I was getting my next high. Being clean behind bars is the worse feeling ever, and no punishment can be enough for what I've done. The nightmares in my head is more punishment than prison could ever be. I can't stop thinking about killing someone as nice as Ms. Vickie. I could never forgive someone for hurting anybody I loved, especially my mother, the way you've forgiven me. I'm really sorry it took me so long to admit this, but I want you to know that I did confess my sins to God and asked for his forgiveness. For the first time in years, I slept peacefully, and whatever life God has left for me, I want to try and get to know him.

It was several months after I received the letter from Tiree that Ms. Beesy called to say thank you. She went on to state that Tiree was released on parole. He seemed to have a hope that she'd not seen in him before about death. He peacefully made his transition.

I felt compelled to help free others from the bondage of deep hurt. This experience led to me incorporating his letter into a sermon about forgiveness. I knew this was a test and God was about to use me in an awesome way. It would not be without many struggles and challenges, but a change was taking place inside of me. The rage was subsiding and slowly turning into hope.

Imagine if God refused to forgive us for all the wrong we've done? That's a frightening thought for me as I've repeatedly gone against His will. I'm so grateful he's a God of second chances.

I continued praying that God would remove any remaining rage and help channel my energy into serving Him.

This gave me the confidence to locate Bill through the white pages. There was a fierce battle with whether to contact him or not. I could just as well forgive him in my heart and keep it moving. For some reason it was hard to walk away. I picked up the phone and dialed the number.

"Hello," the woman who answered the phone stated.

My first thought was to hang up, but I nervously began, "hello is this the home of Bill—," I asked?

"Yes it is," she replied. "Just one moment while I get him."

After a couple minutes, what sounded like an older man picked up the phone. "Hello this is Pastor Bill. How can I help you?"

"Hello sir. My name is Bree and I'm looking for a person by the name of Bill—that was friends with a woman named Vickie Baker. Is that you?"

There was a long pause before Bill responded. "Yes, that would be me."

I took a deep breath before continuing. "This is her daughter, do you know why I'm calling?"

Bill sighed and said, "Yes, I've been anticipating this for some years now. I'm so sorry."

Before he could say anything else, I lost my temper and yelled, "I was a child. Do you have any idea what you stole from me? I was a child! How many other lives did you destroy? How many other children did you molest?"

Bill never answered the question about other children, but while weeping what he did say was "The devil made me do it."

Seriously! "That's your excuse? The devil made you do it! Is that what you've been telling yourself all these years? Does that help you sleep at night and absolve yourself of responsibility? Well you are accountable. Not to me, but God. I pray He has mercy on your tired soul."

Click. I hung up the phone and never spoke to Bill again. Initially, it felt like I failed the test. However, the exchange was not for Bill, but me. It needed to happen so self-forgiveness could occur. It was the beginning of shedding shame and overcoming years of damage. Forgiving Rocky was handled much differently.

I saw Rocky occasionally at funerals or when visiting friends/family in the old neighborhood. It was more beneficial to my mental health to quietly forgive instead of having a confrontation. It wasn't about him, but me being able to empty myself of all the bitterness.

On the other hand, there are some relationships that were just meant to be. Somehow Brad and I reconnected after one of his brother's sons died. Sadly, my anger put too many years between us, and it took a tragedy to bring us back together again. It was as if we never lost contact. There was so much laughter and reminiscing with my brothers about the *good old days*.

It took a long time before I told Brad why our relationship really ended. He was so bothered by how much he'd hurt me even after all these years. Thankfully we were finally able to put all that behind us. New beginnings resulted in a wonderful friendship, which I'm so grateful for.

I was making small strides but determined to keep on the path of forgiveness. I had forgiven Karlos long ago thanks to his mother.

Karlos's mother, Mrs. Rider, and I became really close because we both sung in gospel groups, and she often came to hear me preach. She talked a lot about how I should've been her daughter-in-law. There was also a standing joke that my first child was her grandchild. I always assumed she was talking about Shay, but I'm not so sure anymore.

Mrs. Rider suspected something terrible happened between me and Karlos but insisted she could tell I still loved him. I just told her we grew apart and left it at that. She was right about one thing! There was still love for her son. It was a Phileo type of brotherly/sisterly love. I didn't want to see any harm come to him.

As time went on, I found myself spending more time with Mrs. Rider. One day, she asked me to forgive Karlos for whatever happened between us and to always be there for him. It just came out of nowhere. There was no use trying to convince a mother who knew her child that nothing happened. I assured her Karlos had already been forgiven and I would always be there if he needed me.

Until this day, I've kept that promise. Mrs. Rider made her transition not too long after our conversation. I never knew she was terminally ill.

As for me and Darrell, we are great friends and talk frequently. At first, it was because of the children. Now it's because of my phileo love for him as well. We will always have a bond no matter what life offers. I came to realize he is the father of my children. Not by accident, but together we intentionally conceived and brought them into this world.

To continue harboring any type of ill will against him meant I would have to resent some part of my children. That was unacceptable. I could never look at my children and resent who I chose as their father. They are a major part of my heartbeat, and I never want to have a heart defect.

Darrell's family is also still considered to be a part of my family. I attend various functions when I'm able.

My commitment is to love others, even when it hurts, and not let anger, hatred, and bitterness overtake me again. Do I ever get angry? Absolutely! Honestly, I probably have sinned in my anger, but I've not allowed it to rule over me.

The lesson on forgiveness was a great awakening. It provided a basis for moving in the right direction. The deep-rooted chains of the past were being broken and liberation was occurring.

The ideal of being freed from years of guilt and shame was an awesome feeling. This should have encouraged a channel of consistent communication with God through prayer. I would like to tell you my new-found freedom led to a strong prayer life. I would love to say there were no challenges with mental, physical and spiritual attacks. Nothing is ever that easy.

While I was passionate about the Word, my prayer life was minimal. More time was spent talking to friends than with God. My relationship with Him was surface level. Ultimately the pressures of ministry became too great. I found myself unprepared for all the challenges in the body of Christ and the world. It caused me to step down and leave the church.

I didn't know it then, but this would not be a permanent departure. It took some time to get back into a house of worship but I eventually did. Becoming a member of OLHOP Church, where God planted me. This is where I was to be properly trained and prepared to become the ordained woman of God He created me to be. It took a minute before I stepped back into ministry from fear of failing again. I didn't want to disappoint my Father, who loved me with agape (unconditional) love.

I was more aware of and accepted my strengths and faults. There was a desire never to fail God again. Understanding the flesh is weak it was a promise that couldn't be kept, so I didn't make it.

If we're honest with ourselves, we disappoint Him daily. This experience taught me a valuable lesson. Not even the sincerest believer, no matter position or status, is immune from falling into the traps set for us.

There is hope! David wrote in Psalms 37:23–24 (NIV), "That the Lord makes firm the steps of the one who delights in Him; though he may stumble, he will not fall, for the Lord upholds him with his hand."

The key here is that we delight in Him. He knows we won't always get it right, but we must try. When we disappoint Him, repent, seek forgiveness, and try again with His guidance. This process landed me at OLHOP, where I saw my children begin to flourish.

Shay and CJ loved the church and frequently beat me getting ready on Sundays. CJ was now miming and coming out of her shell, while Shay found her joy in the children's church. OLHOP had its share of problems and wasn't perfect, but no church is.

This is where I experienced a metamorphosis and was challenged to dive deep. Not just to read the Word but to study, digest, and spit it back out.

Pastor "S" was very knowledgeable about the Word and trained his ministers to give seven-minute sermons. The assistant pastor was just as brilliant and knowledgeable and now pastors his own church. Pastor "S" would say, "If you can do it in seven minutes, you can preach anywhere."

He was always full of surprises. We were taught to be prepared with a sermon in our heart. There was no telling when one of us would be called upon to preach.

The pastor and his wife, Lady "T," took me and my children under their wings. I was honored when asked to be the first lady's armor bearer. It was a job that was taken very seriously.

Our friendship quickly grew, and I loved her dearly. There came a time when she was asked to sing at a women's day dinner. Lady "T" had become sick and could hardly speak, let alone sing. When she was called to the podium, I went up and sat directly behind her. Lady "T" opened her mouth to sing, and nothing would come out.

She slightly turned her head to the right, and I immediately knew she was looking for assistance. I stood up and began singing until she could comfortably take lead, at which time I faded out.

At this same event, after the dinner was over, Lady "T" asked me to come into a backroom. She had a surprise for me. I walked into the room, where there were a lot of women standing around in a circle. Lady "T" looked at me and said, "Remember our discussion about you having the desire to speak in tongue?"

I said, "Yes."

"Well we're all here to ask God to baptize you by fire, Lady T proudly exclaimed."

She led me to a chair in the middle of the circle, where I sat as everyone in the room began praying in the spirit. I remember rocking and clenching my mouth shut. My body was shaking like a limb on a tree.

Lady "T" leaned down and said, "You have to open your mouth."

I shook my head no, but she insisted that the only way God could give me the desire of my heart is if I opened my mouth. "He will do the rest," she said.

As my mouth opened, utterances just started pouring out. I tried to stop but it wasn't me. All these words and sounds kept coming and coming. Tears were flowing like a river. I must have spoken to God like that for over forty minutes before slumping over from pure exhaustion.

All the women were clapping, smiling, and crying. Lady "T" leaned down and whispered, "You've just been baptized by fire."

That was it! The gift I was lacking and so desperately desired. God increased my spiritual abilities in a powerful way.

OLHOP was my place of worship until the church closed due to our pastor becoming ill. He returned to his hometown in North Carolina.

I was hurt, but tried not to lose sight of the fact that God saved me from a life of self-destruction. He equipped me with multiple gifts, and put me in the path of men and women who helped strengthen my abilities. For that, I am forever thankful.

Before leaving Michigan, Pastor "S" cautioned me to always be who God called me to be.

He said, "There will be many who fear the gifts God has blessed you with. They will try to hinder you. You're a worshipper and people will try to block you from singing out of fear. You're a preacher and people will try to keep you from preaching. You're a teacher and some will try to prevent you from teaching. You're not a yes person for all the right reasons. This will upset leaders because they'll want to control God's gifts in you. Never become discouraged, and remember that God will make room for your gifts. Keep smiling and whatever you do, make sure it's for the glory of God."

His words were embedded in my memory. Regrettably I found myself without a church home...again!

I kept talking to God, but was like a wanderer in the desert for several years. Trying to find another place of worship, visiting here and there.

An occasion arose when I was driving down a road and happened to see a building out the corner of my eye. It looked like a club house that was associated with the condominium complex next to it. I drove past intending to visit another church when there was a nudge to turn around.

I heard a voice say, "That one!"

"Really, Lord? It doesn't look like a church to me," I said out loud.

Since it was my desire to obey the spirit, I turned around and pulled into the parking lot. There was singing and it didn't sound like any music I was accustomed to.

My first thought was to leave and go to another church, but that didn't happen. After having a few minutes of dialogue with God, I reluctantly got out of my vehicle and went inside the church. There were a few folks who looked like me but I was sure God had made a mistake, knowing that was impossible. I stayed to assess the culture and temperature in the environment.

After service, *I* decided it was not the right place for me and wouldn't be returning. The next Sunday, my intent was to head toward Detroit to visit a place of worship there.

Again, God and I had some back and forth dialogue. I found myself headed in the direction of this church that sat way back off the streets. I must have stayed in the car for about fifteen minutes questioning God and being somewhat defiant before getting out with an attitude.

Most of the people were friendly, but I just didn't understand how God was intending to use me there. My mind quickly reflected on Proverbs 4:5–6. "Trust in the Lord with all your heart and lean not on your own understanding, in all your ways acknowledge Him, and He will direct your paths."

This time, I cleared my mind, closed my eyes and enjoyed the worship team when they began singing. Before long, tears were streaming down my face. I was standing with my arms stretched to God and enjoying being in His presence.

That was a number of years ago when I first walked through the doors of my church.

Once again, my gifts led to working with women and children who had been exposed to childhood sexual abuse, domestic violence and more. My church fully supported and encouraged me in this vision.

God never makes mistakes! Imagine if I had disobeyed His commands, the opportunity to serve His people might have looked a lot different.

Understand that God allows us to face tragedy, hurt, disappointment, and pain so that we can become stronger and look to Him. It takes some of us a long time to find the right path, while others find theirs much sooner in life. It doesn't matter how long the journey is. What matters is arriving at your destination. Once there, fulfill your purpose!

I'm Still Here

Look at me, what do you see? Listen! If you dare.
You want to know what lies beneath the tone of my skin?
What's fighting to be released from the woman within?
Stop! Don't be fooled by what you think you see.
I ain't perfect, I've made plenty bad decisions
Looking for love in all the wrong places
down some long and twisted roads.

My mind was all messed up cause some men got out of control.
Thinking I was ugly cause beauty was something I couldn't see.
Look at me now! Beauty seeps below the depths of my soul.
It explodes through the poetry and music of my words.
A sound still being written and yet to be heard.

Life tried to break me, but bullet proof glass ain't easy to shatter.
Fear tried to overtake my existence and stop me from rising.
But I clapped back at ill intentions and nonsense chatter.
My stature is that of an Amazon woman.
Back straight, head high with a stride of Godly authority.

I walk into a room and command attention with my very presence.
It ain't arrogance, just godly confidence and
representation of my essence.
It's a little bit of boldness and a great lack of fear.
It's a touch of evolution and a dash of "I'm still here."

Chapter 17

Statistically Speaking

Encounter after encounter, my life has been filled with those who were violated by people they knew and loved. Not one was a stranger danger situation. I implore every parent to be observant and engage in open, honest communication with their children. Empower them to feel confident that no matter what or who, they have permission to tell and you will support them.

Fear and shame are tactics that perpetrators use to continue their abuse. Fear and shame are not the victims to carry but the one who inflicted the pain.

I've talked a lot about how childhood sexual abuse and trauma have an Impact on behaviors and how we build relationships. Let's take a moment to discuss the definition and possible characteristics that are frequently associated with this type of trauma.

How Is Child Sexual Abuse Defined?

Amazingly there is no clear answer to this question, but to help readers understand, a simplified definition was obtained from the *National Child Traumatic Stress Network*: "any interaction between a child and an adult (or another child of significant age difference) in which the child is used for the sexual stimulation of the perpetrator or an observer. Sexual abuse can include both touching and non-touching behaviors. Touching behaviors may involve touching of the vagina, penis, breasts or buttocks, oral-genital contact, or sexual intercourse. Non-touching behaviors can include voyeurism (trying to look at a child's naked body), exhibitionism, or exposing the child to pornography."

Many perpetrators don't start their abuse by using physical force. Instead they use methods, such as grooming.

The United States Department of Justice (USDOJ), Office of Sex Offender Sentencing, Monitoring, Apprehending, and Tracking (SMART) indicate that many child sexual abusers build a trusting relationship with a child to manipulate him/her into compliance with the sexual act. Perpetrators also tend to have/build a trusting relationship with the parents/caregivers of children to gain access and time alone with them.

The prevalence of child sexual abuse is difficult to determine because assaults frequently go unreported. Depending on the source, it is estimated that about one in every six girls and one in every ten boys have/will be exposed to sexual assault by their eighteenth birthday. Experts agree that the rate of actual child sexual abuse is much higher due to lack of reporting.

What Are the Signs of Abuse?

Knowledge is our best defense to protecting children. While the information below was obtained from SMART's website, many of these behaviors can show up in children for multiple reasons and does not necessarily mean that sexual abuse has occurred. The information is primarily to assist with recognizing concerning behaviors so the appropriate action can be taken.

Behaviors typically found in younger children:

1. Nightmares or other sleep problems without an explanation
2. Seems distracted or distant at odd times
3. Sudden change in appetite (increase or decrease)

4. Sudden mood swings: rage, fear, insecurity or withdrawal
5. Leaves *clues* that are likely to provoke a discussion about sexual issues
6. New or unusual fear of certain people or places
7. Refusal to talk about a secret shared with an adult or older child
8. Writes, draws, plays, or dreams of sexual or frightening images
9. Talks about a new older friend
10. Suddenly has money, toys, or other gifts without reason
11. Thinks of self or body as repulsive, dirty, or bad
12. Exhibits new adult-like sexual behaviors, language, and knowledge
13. Has physical signs of sexual abuse (these are more rare but may include the following):
    a. Pain, bleeding, discharge, or other physical trauma to the genitals, anus, or mouth
    b. Vaginal infections (girls) or sexually transmitted diseases
    c. Persistent or recurring pain during urination or bowel movements
    d. Wetting or soiling accidents unrelated to toilet training
    e. Trouble swallowing

Behaviors more typically found in teens:

- Signs of depression or anxiety
- Self-harming behaviors (cutting, burning)
- Suicidal thoughts or attempts
- Compulsive eating or dieting
- Inadequate personal hygiene
- Drug and alcohol abuse
- Sexual promiscuity
- Running away from home
- Fear of intimacy or closeness
- Extra money or gifts without explanation

The Child Welfare Information Gateway indicates that "all States include sexual abuse in their definitions of child abuse. Some States refer in general terms to sexual abuse, while others specify various acts as sexual abuse.

Sexual exploitation is an element of the definition of sexual abuse in most jurisdictions and includes allowing a child to engage in prostitution or in the production of child pornography.

In about thirty-three (33) States, the definition of sexual abuse includes human trafficking, sex trafficking or trafficking of children for sexual purposes."

In my opinion, the best thing we can do to arm our children is provide them with knowledge. That's why it's important to teach children the anatomically correct name for describing their private areas (e.g. penis, vagina, buttocks, breasts) as early as when it's age-appropriate to do so. Possibly at the same time, you begin teaching them about their fingers, hands, nose, toes, etc., around the age of two or so, but every child is different.

I'm not a licensed therapist, psychologist or psychiatrist, so please check with your child's doctor or another professional if you need help.

I know it's more comfortable for us to come up with nicknames like *weiner, pee pee, cookie,* or *pocketbook* because we don't want to be humiliated when our young children make a public announcement that their penis or vagina itches. If you're a parent, you know what I'm talking about, except they yell out the cute nicknames we gave them.

Why do I think this is important? I've come across a number of teens who still refer to their private body parts in terms of nicknames learned during early childhood. This can be even more embarrassing when a younger child makes a public announcement. Additionally, if a younger child discloses sexual abuse and an investigation is initiated, small children need to be able to correctly identify which part of their body was violated.

This can sometimes be very confusing for younger children and untrained adults. Let me give a brief example. Suppose a law enforcement officer, who is unfamiliar with interviewing young children, is dispatched to a home for a domestic disturbance. He (Officer Joe) and three other officers discover that a four-year old little girl (Pella) was allegedly sexually assaulted by her mother's boyfriend. The mother was homicidal and screaming she wanted to press charges.

Officer Joe decides to speak with Pella on the spot in the presence of a female colleague (Officer Val), away from the adults. The other two officers are taking a report from the adults regarding the domestic disturbance.

Officer Joe steps into the room where Pella is sitting on her bed while Officer Val waits by the door. Officer Joe asks Pella her name before introducing himself.

He states, "Mommy's really upset, huh?"

Pella nods her head yes without speaking.

Officer Joe is very gentle and caring as he has small talk with Pella but visibly uncomfortable with the line of questioning he's about to begin.

Officer Val states, "Maybe it would be better if I talked to Pella."

Officer Joe declines and proceeds with his interview. He's about 6'1" and chose to stand over Pella while she sat on her bed. Pella was noticeably afraid of him, but he continued to stand as he stated:

"I'm told you were hurt by someone. Can you tell me where you were hurt?"

Pella is shaking, crying, and cringing as she's barely able to say, in a low gurgled voice, "My pocketbook."

Officer Joe barely understands and takes a step toward her while stating, "Did you say you want your pocketbook? I'll have someone get it for you when we're done, is that okay?"

Officer Val attempted to intervene, but Officer Joe put his hand up indicating for her to stop.

Pella started screaming and wanted Officer Joe to move away from her. He appeared confused and had no idea the mistakes he'd just made.

Officer Val had some experience with talking to children and quietly asked Office Joe to step out of the room as she privately handed him her gun.

Officer Joe moved back toward the bedroom door and observed.

Officer Val squatted to become eye level with Pella and asked, "Is it okay if I sit here with you?"

Sniffling and still shaken, Pella said yes.

Officer Val's tone of voice was soft and soothing. She began talking to Pella about her dolls and other items in her room. After about twenty minutes, Officer Val asked Pella if she knew the difference between the truth and a lie.

Pella nodded her head yes.

Officer Val responded, "So if I said your dolls hair is red, would that be the truth or a lie?"

Pella smiled and said, "That's a lie because her hair is black."

"What if I said your dolls hair is short, would that be the truth or a lie?"

Pella responded, "That's the truth."

Officer Val said, "You're absolutely correct. Now I need to ask you another question. This time, I want to ask you if you know why we're here?"

Pella quietly said, "Because Mommy's mad at Buster."

Officer Val, asked Pella, do you know why Mommy is mad at Buster?

"Because he touched my pocketbook," Pella replied.

"Can you tell me where your pocketbook is?" Officer Val inquired.

Pella had become comfortable and blushed as she slightly spread her legs and pointed to her vagina.

Needless to say, Officer Joe realized his mistakes and learned a valuable lesson. This is a lesson for all parents as well. Arm your children with correct terminology to empower them and minimize confusion.

Anytime you become suspicious that a child may need help, please speak up. If you suspect something, say something! Any concerned citizen can report suspected child abuse and/or neglect by calling your state's child protection team and/or police department. Find out your state's child protective service contact information and make it a part of your list of emergency numbers.

Also, keep in mind that there are some individuals who are mandated reporters and required by law to report any suspicions of child abuse/neglect. This includes, but is not limited to medical professionals, mental health professionals, law enforcement, teachers, clergy, childcare providers, social workers, and others. Everyone has a responsibility to help stop the abuse of children.

Sometimes in life, we find ourselves in all kinds of situations. There are those we have little control over and others we take control of. The latter has not always resulted in good choices. The following prayer is specifically for women seeking to be strengthened. Find ten minutes in your day and have a talk with God. If you've always been lost for words, let this prayer guide you.

The Heart of a Praying Woman

Lord, I thank you for coming from heaven to earth to die on the cross for my sins and the sins of my forefathers. In your precious name, I thank you for my ancestors who endured self-sacrifice, which ultimately led to the shedding of their blood, that I might have a better life.

I thank you for my parents who loved me enough to conceive and give life. They could have easily chosen to discard of me. I thank you for other strong men and women of God, some known and others unknown, who you placed in my life to guide and direct my path.

I thank you for the struggles of life as a child and as an adult. If not for those struggles, I would not know how to conquer my demons and overcome my challenges.

Thank you for the knowledge that I am no longer a victim of past tragedies but a victor over every circumstance. Thank you for rescuing me from my own self-destructive thoughts and actions.

Because of you, oh God, I am learning to push through hurt and pain despite my desire to withdraw and hide my face. I will no longer be held captive by shame or fear. I know that the Lord is my light, and dark forces shall pass over me. Why should I be afraid? I will speak on your behalf and not be afraid because I know that you are with me.

Thank you for freeing me and all those I love from negative spirits that spread from one generation to the next. In Jesus's name, I break any generational curses that have been cast against me and my family. I rebuke alcoholism, drug abuse, premature death, molestation, mental illness, violence, or any other form of brokenness.

I will be cautious not to allow my mind to become lured into bondage and will deny my flesh that I may be free from invisible shackles that have in times past prevented me from boldly seeking and carrying out my purpose. Thank you for helping me understand that Satan's main objective on this earth is to kill my spirit, steal my heart, and destroy my mind.

I ask forgiveness for all my sins. I provide no excuses for the wrong I've done throughout my life. Forgive me when my actions have brought harm to others.

By the power of your might, I will strive to protect my temple and keep it clean, holy, and acceptable unto you, oh Lord. Help my mind to be focused on that which pleases you.

I will not subject myself to emotional turmoil that causes me to fall away from you. I will carefully choose those whom I allow into my life. I understand that everyone who acts good to me is not necessarily good for me. I know that everything that replicates diamonds doesn't always shine. Bind my fleshly desire and put it under submission.

If you desire a mate for me, he will be a Godly man. Someone waiting to give and receive love. We will hold each other in high esteem. Together our spirits become one and seek to please you. Help us put you first Lord, making it difficult to be easily drawn from the sanctity of our marriage. Our spirit will reject any relationship that seeks to destroy our bond with you and each other

Lord, my future husband and I will be delivered from life-long anger, shame and self-hatred. We'll come together with softened hearts, to give and receive affection. Our mantra will be rooted in "first, do no harm."

Our goal will always be to put you first. Breaking any familial strongholds holding us captive. I declare spiritual, mental, emotional, and financial stability. We shall become one with you. Our children will be raised knowing who you are.

If I am already married, Lord I confess that during times of anger, I've withheld my affections. There are days when I've felt his attention and passion has turned from me to something or someone else. Have I faded into the background of his heart? I began to wonder, "Do I matter?"

I understand there is nothing you cannot do. No relationship you cannot heal. I place my marriage in your hands. Lead and guide me with your strength and wisdom.

Lord if I am a single woman, help me to become one with you. I surrender to your headship of my life. You are my provider, friend and protector of my heart.

I am true to myself in knowing that fleshly desires are strong and real. I confess that my body goes through phases where it yearns to be held. To simply know that I exist and matter to someone. I question, "Who do I belong to and who belongs to me?"

Father, forgive me if I have lost myself in the world and coveted that which was not meant for me. Filling my life with people and things in an effort to replace an empty void. Oh God, I cry out and call on your name to give me wisdom and understanding.

Thank you for bringing me into the knowledge that I am beautifully, uniquely, and wonderfully made. I matter to you. I am important to the building of your kingdom. Although woman was created from man, man is born of woman. I am a daughter of the King, the most-high God, joint heir to the throne. In the kingdom, I shall never want nor shall my heart be troubled concerning my living.

I shall always have a home because the Word informs me that in my Father's house, there are many mansions. Yes, I matter. I am someone of great regard as my net worth is immeasurable. Not because of who man perceives me to be, but because of who you called and predestined me to be.

Father, I am not foolish and understand that the enemy wants me to jeopardize my covering. He is shrewd and entices me to risk the protection of all those I love by turning a death ear and blind eye to my first love.

I receive my appointment to be an intercessor for others. As a mother, I will be the shero to my children. I will raise them in the admonition of the Lord, teaching them all that is right and good. I will train them up in the way that a child should go so that when they are away from me, they are never far from their covering. They shall always seek your face in good times and bad. If I have no children, as a sister, aunt, grandmother, neighbor, or friend, I commit to being a godly example to children I love in the absence of their parents.

I claim victory over seen and unseen entities. I am strong and have entered into a state of warfare. I battle the enemy with the Sword of the spirit. I commit to drawing others unto you by manifesting your Word. What was dead in me is now alive. Any negative thoughts that try to makes its home in me shall be rebuked.

Strengthen me to be a godly woman in my home, on my job, in the church and wherever I go. Allow others to see you in me.

Forgive me when I've yelled at my children for sharing differences of opinion because you gave them breath. Forgive me when I've complained about the pressures of my job. It was you who assured that the position I hold was created just for me. Forgive me for not standing strong or giving into peer pressure when faced with adversities.

I want to be one of your faithful workers recruited as a full-time disciple. Commissioned to post Help Wanted signs all over the face of this earth. Lord, you are mighty, and through you, I commit to tearing down strongholds, casting down every imagination that is not of you. Help me to hold fast to the good fight of faith. Looking neither to the left or right but having tunnel vision with my eyes stayed on you.

Oh Lord, you've made me a stronger person because of who you are. I don't want to take one step, one breath, or make one move without you as my inspiration. I want to be more like you. Instill within me a clean and forgiving heart, a listening ear, and a nurturing tongue.

If I have harmed others with my words, acts, or deeds, let my pride not have dominion over me. Help me to seek forgiveness.

In the name of Jesus and by His might, I thank you for the predestination of the ministry you have in me. Understanding where I came from in this earthly life. Though I live in this world, I am not of it. I remove myself from anything or anyone that discourages my spiritual growth. I will not subject myself to false teachings or worship the material things of this world.

I accept my charge to shed the old woman so the new one may be properly fed. Having been weaned from milk and now chewing on meat. I understand this is necessary for the proper development of my mind and spirit. Your word is strengthening me to follow the path you've paved.

I thank you Lord for helping me overcome the mindset of economic impoverishment. For conquering the mental division of class and race, because I am rich in all things. I am a first-class servant of the Lord. I race to the finish line of royalty. I surrender myself completely to you and cast down any spirit not of you. Whether it is jealously, covetousness, animosity, gossip, or backbiting. I bind its effects on my family, friends, and fellow believers.

Today I release into my environment commitment, self-determination, self-sacrifice, and humility. I will do everything possible to fight for what is right. When I have done all I can to withstand, give me the courage to just *stand*.

I know that in my standing, at times, I will stand alone and be judged unfairly. My reward is not acceptance by man, but by you, oh God.

I know that as I strive to maintain my godly walk, true believers will receive me. Unbelievers and those who profess to believe will reject me. I will frequently be misunderstood. When acts of kindness are misconstrued, abused, or misinterpreted, I will not become offended. I have no doubt that any weapon that rises against me will not flourish. Every tongue coming against me in judgment will be ruined.

Lord, I am your willing vessel, eager to please you as young children strive to please their parents. I have become full, with the fruit of life. Each day, I will examine myself whether I be in the faith. I will not unfairly judge others, and during those times when I have ill feelings against my brother or sister, I will go to them in love. When my mind becomes cluttered with angry and vengeful thoughts, I will meditate and pray.

I know that your grace is sufficient, and your strength is made perfect in weakness. There are no perfect beings outside of you, oh Lord, that have walked the face of this earth. May I faithfully and consistently strive for perfection to display more of you and less of me. I know that whatever is asked in your name shall be given to me. When I kneel down and fall prostrate before you, may my prayers be unselfish in nature and my motives pure.

Thank you for your light, grace, and mercy. I ask that your angels encamp round about me and all those I love, placing a shield of protection around us. Thank you for the inspiration of this prayer and your agape (unconditional) love. In Jesus's name, amen.

Charge It to My Account

Mother, you carried the weight of the world on your shoulders. You were so strong and steadfast. Sacrificing much of your happiness to assure a better life for the children you loved so deeply. I never gave up because you pushed me to be a winner. I've become strong because you never let me give into my weaknesses.

I have learned to build on my strengths and strive to improve my faults because you would accept no less. I will not forget the lessons you taught because you loved me enough to be my teacher. I am because you were, what I hope to be, the epitome of motherhood. I can now credit my charge accounts because of what you have instilled in me.

Because of you, Mother, and your belief in me, I threw away the card that labeled me unattractive according to society's definition of beauty. I replaced that card with a positive self-worth account and charged it to the limit.

I walk with my head held high and my back straight with two-inch heels as the curve of my hips and the depths of my thighs accessorize my inner beauty.

I cut up my nonbeliever's card and charged the balance to my faith account to guide me through my order of priority: God, family; God, friends; God, church; God, employment; God.

God is the creator of my destiny. I will not surrender my mind to the temptations of greed, dishonesty, and selfishness. Mother, you endured hardships of the past, which gave me credit for the present. My future was paid for in advance through your love and encouragement. My fate was sealed with the death of our Lord and Savior, Jesus Christ.

Finally, Mother, I closed out my fear account and opened five accounts worth one million in courage. You have always been by my side, in the shadows, watching, waiting, praying, and crying. Hoping that all your hard work would someday pay off.

Watch no more, Mother! Wait not another second! Relax your tired hands and allow me to wipe the tears from your eyes. Thank you for giving me the courage to love and be loved. Mother, if there are any charges I neglected to purchase, please, charge it to the account of my head and not my heart.

Moonlight and Friendship (To Sue)

Our friendship is like a glowing moon in the evening sky.
After the sun has set and night quickly surrounds day,
the glare of moonlight beams with encouragement.
She is often seen with a smile warming the hearts of all
those that marvel at her beauty.
The mind is left to wonder, where does moonlight receive the
tenacity to fight through the dreary nights.
She returns over and over again with the ability to shine
upon the darkest of life's challenges.

My heart is filled with joy when I see her mouth open with praise.
The eyes of moonlight radiate with hope even when
the rain pours out upon her.
She has battled against the greatest of storms to simply
show up and be moonlight.
During days of pure exhaustion, she never ceases to
burst through the dark clouds.

Moonlight brings rays of glimmer that seep deep into
the essence of her existence.
The power of her brightness is so great that it holds
back the shadows of gloomy days.
Finally, I hear the calmness of her voice as we quietly agree…
Where I go, together we go!

That's moonlight and friendship!

Never say Never!

This book is mostly about early childhood trauma, it's effect on behavior and my journey to an authentic relationship with God. It discusses many associations with various people. However, the book intentionally does not reflect more current aspects of my life such as a second marriage, grandchildren and more.
Maybe that's a book for another time.

Stay Tuned…

About the Author

S.L. Baker was born and raised in Detroit, Michigan. Her parents separated when she was very young, but she describes her family unit as "totally complete" despite not meeting the world's view of a nuclear family.

Baker obtained her Bachelor's in Social Work and Master's in Human Resource Administration.

She is a strong advocate for children's rights and has over 30-years of experience working on behalf of children and families. This is not by accident but by design. Baker's exposure to trauma, like many, began at a very young age. Tragedy in her life seemed to spiral out of control to the point of hopelessness. Somehow her pain was transformed into purpose, which led to activism for children.

Baker now has two beautiful daughters and is a licensed pastor. She dedicates her life to educating children, families, communities and congregations on the impact of trauma. She has presented at seminars, workshops, faith-based organizations, schools, professional groups, and to the general public. Her calling did not come without many tragedies and challenges but was birth despite her circumstances.

Throughout the years, Baker's lifelong advocacy has been recognized by various groups for outstanding leadership. This includes the Lakeshore Optimist club, Michigan's Department of Health and Human Services and other human service organizations, The Alliance for a Safer Greater Detroit, The Detroit Board of Police Commissioners, Detroit City Council, Detroit Chief of Police and more.